Incredible Divorce

MIND OVER MATTER

MARK ANTHONY

Order this book online at www.trafford.com
or email orders@trafford.com

Most Trafford titles are also available at major online book retailers.

Scripture quotations marked KJV are from the Holy Bible, King James Version
(Authorized Version). First published in 1611. Quoted from the KJV Classic
Reference Bible, Copyright © 1983 by The Zondervan Corporation.

Print information available on the last page.

ISBN: 978-1-4907-9743-4 (sc)
ISBN: 978-1-4907-9745-8 (hc)
ISBN: 978-1-4907-9744-1 (e)

Library of Congress Control Number: 2019914402

Trafford rev. 11/14/2019

 www.trafford.com

North America & international
toll-free: 1 888 232 4444 (USA & Canada)
fax: 812 355 4082

Contents

The Inspiration Behind This Book

I WENT TO VISIT MY DENTIST, and just out of a conversation, we started to talk about divorce. He had been through his already, and I was already getting started to set in motion my own divorce proceedings. In fact, I already had in mind at the time the right attorney and how much money I would need to get myself out of this mess. He told me about how he had spent so much money for his attorney's fees. He told me about how he had wasted money on one attorney and had to get another. The dollars he had spent was in the thousands. Right then, what went through my head was I didn't have the kind of money he did; and if he lost his battle in court, I knew I would lose mine as well. Right then and there, I realized that depending on the power of the dollar and the skills of an attorney weren't the key. I had to take a different approach.

The seed of defeat was being planted in my mind. My dentist went on to say he had another dentist friend who had just gone through a divorce and now had to pay his wife's maintenance costs for the rest of her life, because his wife had never worked a day in her life and had no skills other than being a housewife. I still refused to let the word *defeat* take control of my mind. Still, I would talk positive, as though my battle had already been won with a verse on my mind, Proverbs 18:21 Death and Life are in the power of the tongue. My dentist would just look at me, as if to say, *Yeah, right.* Instead, he would give me a low-key smile. It was as though our justice system was tailor-made to rule in my wife's favor under the circumstances of her being on social security and being unable to work.

With no doubt, I knew what was going on in my dentist's mind: my wife was going to eat me up in court. But he didn't have the heart to tell me so. I could read right through his thoughts. *Here's a woman, with a disability, with no income, and unable to work, and you expect not to take care of her for the rest of her life.* He didn't want to burst my bubble, so he just remained silent; and when the time came, I would see for myself. It wasn't only my dentist who thought that way; everyone else had the same attitude: I was fighting a losing battle.

No one had anything positive to say in my defense, and they would laugh and mumble behind my back. When I say no one, I mean no one could see a light at the end of my tunnel. I could tell my dentist knew the odds were against me—not because of my gender or my race, but because of the circumstances that lay before me.

It was even more of a challenge for me because no one believed I would defeat my wife in court. I started to distance myself from negative people who were trying to discourage me from pursuing the things they thought were impossible. Their negative thoughts motivated me even more. I just refused to be under the influence of others who at one time had lost their case in court, or knew someone who did. I simply refused to reward my wife for the abuse she had put my kids through and the hardship she had caused me with my relatives, especially with my sister Sally. I had so much hate for her within me.

During my follow-up visits to my dentist, I would give him a little update on my divorce case. It appeared as though he was just waiting for me to tell him how my wife had chewed me up in court, but I informed him that no decision had been made yet. My dentist's low-key smile gave me the impression that he was waiting for the judge to pull the plug, because I was doomed anyway. The only life support system I had was my own beliefs.

Don't believe anyone who tells you that going through a divorce isn't stressful. I knew I had to conquer my fear and overrule the thoughts of others; I had no time to deal with an idle mind. The way I saw it, if an armed intruder entered my home to take my life, would it be wise for me to fight (knowing the odds was against me), or should I just let him kill me without putting up a struggle? In my mind, it was my life that was at stake here.

My wife's goal was to financially take my life, driven as she was by her greed. Well, what was so amazing was the outcome of my divorce hearing. Upon telling my dentist of the judge's ruling, his mouth just dropped open, and his expression was one of amazement. The first thing he said was, "You need to write a book."

I didn't take him seriously when he told me this. It's a fact that you can actually make the world turn, if you just applied yourself. Every time I went to see my dentist, he would always say, "You need to write a book. Your book could be a consolation to someone else."

Slowly but surely, he started to convince me. For many of months, I wrestled with myself. I had no interest in writing this book, but then again, my dentist really inspired me to write it. What you read in this book is a true story of my marriage and my divorce.

This book wasn't written for a specific gender or race, but for anyone who feels he or she is trapped and sees no way out. When I looked at all the angles and saw no open doors, no gaps, the odds being too much against me, I looked deep within myself and was introduced to my inner spirit, which was just waiting to take control. Anger was put on the side, because patience and planning were the key. I had to clear my mind of negative thoughts and separate myself from negative people. My wife's battle against me was yet to be won.

I hope this book will encourage someone else that there's hope, if one is willing to acknowledge it, and realize that negative thoughts have no place in the courtroom.

CHAPTER 1

Marriage and Divorce

MARRIAGE IS A JOURNEY INTO the unknown. You never know where it may lead and what hardships you will encounter, which may leave a bitter taste in your mouth. It may be a temporary or a lifetime commitment. Many of us enter into a marriage for love, others for personal gain or for other reasons. Perhaps many marriages are a great investment; and for some, it's like investing in the wrong stock, which could be a total loss.

Some marriages can best be described as a candlelight marriage—full of fire at the beginning, but soon it will burn out, with less smiles, multiplying and dividing itself between love and hate. A marriage can be filled with lust, greed, and discrimination. It can be more "Do as I say, not as I do"; accepting the better and leaving the worse; and taking away the love and leaving nothing but pain, sorrow, and hate. Marriage is not just marrying the individual; it's also being faithful to the vows made before God. Many people feel trapped in their marriage and don't know which way to turn, and are intimidated by the thought of what their spouse may take from them.

Many have accepted the facts of living with domestic violence—fighting that could escalate into fatal stabbings or shootings. Some people are trapped in abusive marriages for years, others a lifetime; some resort to committing suicide as a way out.

What's even more devastating is when a child has to live in an environment of domestic violence. Scared to death, their hearts beating like a drum, trembling with fear, being blinded by their own tears, anxious over being made to witness the verbal and physical abuse their parents inflict on each other fighting like cats and dogs. Exposed to this, a helpless, innocent child is now scarred—for life. Nevertheless, for many, a line must be drawn to avoid greater hardships in the years to come.

However, domestic violence cannot be used in court in a divorce case to influence a judge's decision. Physical force can get you incarcerated from one to three years, giving your spouse grounds for a divorce, depending on the laws of the state you live in.

Incarceration is a legitimate ground for divorce in many states, including New Jersey, Texas, Pennsylvania, and Maryland. A marriage has its own reasons for taking place, and every marriage has its own destiny—some for life, and some for a price.

You may have heard of the advice "To find a good wife or a good husband, find them in church," but I say this: both of my wives were churchgoing women and claimed to have been saved and sanctified. However, they saved their lies for their advantage. Acting under the influence of other people as to whom you should or shouldn't marry has left many separated from their spouses, divorced, even dead—just because they chose to go through the motions, bearing a title and accepting things just the way they are. Many people are like a fish: they'll bite at almost anything and end up on a hook. Follow your own heart.

Entering into a marriage for the wrong reasons gets no approval from God, who wants nothing other than for married couples to love and cherish each other for the rest of their lives. Marrying someone is no different from giving a homeless person a dime: if it doesn't come from the heart, your giving is in vain and has no value. Marriage is not about the material things one can gain but about gaining a heart, which is priceless. When all the material things are gone, the heart still stands, even if it has to stand alone.

Divorce is a word that suggests being free; but in some cases, being free can be very costly. Many people feel that going to divorce court can be very intimidating, because of the word *defeat*. Many people are already defeated even before the proceedings, because the seed has already been planted in their minds by a friend, a neighbor, or a relative who had been in the same situation and lost the battle in court.

Thinking positive can cause good things to happen; on the other hand, negative thoughts can poison the mind and destroy you. The word *defeat* penetrates the minds of those who self-destruct.

A divorce battle in court can get very ugly—no holds barred. Hitting below the belt is perfectly legal. Many people have opted to stay in their marriage for different reasons—for money, inheritance, personal property, maintenance, child support, or just for the kids' sake, or even for their religious beliefs. Marriage has always been a battle of understanding and trust; both parties play a combination in a good marriage. And having one without the other is a time bomb just waiting to go off.

We have heard the phrase "let freedom ring" without really knowing what freedom means in our own home. Many are still living in slavery—being a slave in their own home, not because of the color of their skin but the mismatched colors that make up their characters, turning them into a slave servant in their marriage, and their marriage is put on a shelf and preserved for many reasons.

In most cases, people stay in a bad marriage until they've reached their limit, until they feel they just can't take any more. And feeling like an overloaded fuse that's about to blow, angry and expecting an attorney to pull a rabbit out of a hat. It's been proven that money can't buy a person everything. Many wealthy people can't be bothered to clean up their own mess. They're choked and blinded by it, but they lack the time or knowledge to deal with it, so they use the power of the dollar and leave their lives in the hands of lawyers.

However, every divorce case is different, and no attorney knows your spouse better than you do. Your attorney can only prepare your case based on what you tell him, and he will apply his knowledge according to the law. Understanding your case plays a major factor in the result. Nevertheless, having a good attorney guiding you through the legal hurdle is very important, so make sure you have a good one, someone who has your best interest at heart and is not just interested in what he or she can squeeze out from your wallet.

You would be amazed by how many attorneys an individual goes through in the course of a divorce case. Finding the right attorney can be very difficult. Many talk a good game, drawing a picture no artist can draw, convincing you that he can conquer the world, until he has conquered your mind and drained your wallet dry. A terrible attorney can destroy your determination to fight, elevating your anger, lessening your desire to pursue your case, planting the idea of defeat in your mind.

Number one rule: Never enter into a divorce filled with anger. Anger will destroy you.

If a fighter enters the ring filled with anger, swinging wildly and without any strategy, and struggling and hoping to land the right punch, his opponent is going to knock him out. Don't be an angry fighter. The sea may get a little rough, but stay focused, and stay on course. Use your anger as a leveling tool; use it to your advantage to defeat your opponent.

Never enter a courtroom with only a verbal agreement with your spouse. Always have a written statement covering the verbal agreement. In court, a verbal agreement is your word against your spouse. The tables might turn with some underhanded dealings that would take you totally by surprise, leaving you without any sound defense.

Always be prepared for the worst. You need to keep your homework and important documents at your fingertips. No matter how large or how small in value your documents may seem to you at the time, file them in alphabetical order for easy access in court. Digging for your documents in court is a reflection of you digging your own grave.

Always be prepared for anything that might come up. Hang on to those documents that track your spouse's life—from the day they were born to the present: birth certificate, school records, current light bill, rent receipts, paycheck stubs (showing proof of income and ability to work), proof of employment or self-employment, even canceled checks from employers, proof of retirement benefits, proof of medical benefits such as Medicare, and any health insurance papers. Proof of medical benefits can entitle you to benefits outlined in a law called the COBRA

(Consolidated Omnibus Budget Reconciliation Act), along with banks statements, social security benefits, etc. Remember, don't take anything for granted.

The judge has the first and last say in your divorce case. It's very important to make a great impression. Your first impression could be your last. Prepare your case in a professional manner, with documents to back up all your statements. Getting the judge's interest will open doors in the judge's mind and introduce doubts as to your spouse, allowing you to take your case even farther.

With the right documents, you can destroy your spouse's credibility, and destroying their credibility is the number one key to influencing the judge's decision.

How can a mechanic properly fix a vehicle without the proper tools? Your documents are the tools you need to fix the problem. They could help you avoid the hassle of maintenance for months, or even for a lifetime. As I said, having the proper documents is a very important factor in how your case goes in court. He says or she says has no bearing in the courtroom.

Never be too quick to answer questions. An attorney has many verbal tricks up his sleeves. Think before answering anything. Make sure you understand the question. And if for any reason you do not understand the question being asked, all you have to say are six little words: *I do not understand the question.*

Chapter 2

Robert's Childhood

ROBERT WAS BORN IN New Orleans, Louisiana; and a short time after his birth, his father and his mother took him and his two sisters to live with their grandmother in a town called Jackson Mississippi, north of New Orleans. That is to say, when Robert was born, he was born with something called the widow's peak.

The widow's peak is a V shape at the center of the hairline. When Robert was a child, his auntie told him the widow's peak meant he would never be able to keep a wife. As far as Robert was concerned, his auntie was just teasing him, out of superstition.

Robert thought the widow's peak meant he would never be able to keep a wife long enough; people said the widow's peak simply meant he would outlive his wife. When Robert was in the second grade, his parents decided it was best for him and his sisters, Julie and Sally, to return to New Orleans to attend school. Their father felt the school in Mississippi wasn't advanced enough to give them the best education they needed.

But little did Robert's father know that Robert was the clown of the class. Robert was very disturbed about going to school in New Orleans, because the school in Mississippi was the only school he knew, and he hated the thought of leaving his cousins behind and going back to the place where he was born but had no memories of. Going to school in New Orleans was very troubling for Robert and his sisters. Not a day would pass when their classmates would not make fun of them, calling them country.

Robert never took his education seriously, until he wasn't promoted to the third grade. After that, he realized he needed to apply himself, because he didn't want to be left behind. He started to realize how important his education really was, and he refused to repeat another grade ever again.

At this point, he had no idea where his journey would lead him, growing up a little too fast and taking on responsibilities that would deny him his childhood and his education.

It all started when he wanted to be a trouble-free child, which meant he never wanted to ask his parents for anything, knowing it was a struggle for them just to keep a roof over their heads, food on the table, and shoes on their feet. So at a very early age, Robert would make money cutting grass with his father, who paid him a dollar a day. He would save his money in a shoebox under his bed.

Things were cheaper then. A quarter would buy him a whole bag of candy. He could get a soda for only 15 cents and a gallon of gas for something between thirty and thirty five cents. Robert's father bought him only one jacket, and from that point on, Robert bought his own school clothes and supplies. He made a dollar any way he could and never depended on his parents for anything under any circumstances.

He later became a paperboy, which he didn't like at all. A short time later, he worked at a drugstore as a delivery boy, riding a bike to take medication to customers And he stayed in school. However, juggling school and work, he never got a chance to attend a football or basketball game in his entire student life. Even in the worst of weather, he would work; at times he would come home soaking wet.

Robert got out of school at three fifteen and had to report to work at three thirty. His schedule didn't allow him to do much of anything but go to school and work; he had very little time for homework. Each morning he would get up for school after having had only a few hours of sleep. Some mornings he would oversleep, too tired to respond to the alarm clock. Eventually, he started missing his classes, or skipping schooldays altogether.

And each time he missed school, the school would mail a letter to his parents to let them know about it. His parents never saw the letters because he would take them out of the mailbox and get rid of them.

His attendance got so bad he ended up missing ninety-nine days of school. He would report only on test days. He was called to the office by his counselor, who warned him that if he missed one more day of school, he was going to be expelled.

From the look in his counselor's eyes, Robert knew she was serious; and getting kicked out of school was the last thing he needed. In his mind, he kept telling himself he couldn't miss another day, and he determined he would do whatever it took not to oversleep again. The very next day, he got up for school, after barely getting any rest, too paranoid of oversleeping.

Robert went back to his old routine of working long hours, coming home, getting his homework done, and then neglecting himself again with only a few hours of sleep. One morning, he found himself waking up exhausted from oversleeping again, which meant one more absence from school. In the back of his mind, all he could hear was his counselor's warning: if he missed one more day, he would be expelled from school. When he got up for school the next morning, he was very nervous, hoping his counselor wouldn't expel him from school.

After being in school all day, he finally felt that maybe his counselor didn't catch his absence, so he started to feel a little relaxed. Until his teacher informed him his counselor wanted to see him in her office.

As he walked down the long hallway, his heart was beating like a drum. He listened to his own footsteps echoing each step he took, remembering his counselor's every word. His body felt totally weak, and his hands were shaking. He knew he would be expelled, and he did not know how he was going to keep this from his parents.

He entered his counselor's office very slowly, acting clueless, playing dumb, but knowing he had done something wrong. All he could hear in his mind was her saying, *Go, clean out your locker, because as of today, you no longer attend this school.* Instead, she looked at him as if to say, *Robert, a mind is a terrible thing to waste.* Out loud she said, "How can you come to school only on test days and then pass all your tests when other kids who come here every day fail theirs? I just can't understand that."

She continued, "For this reason, I can't just expel you from school." She looked at him with an expression of great sadness. "Robert, you are too smart to throw your education down the drain."

Robert knew what she was saying was true. But he felt trapped between his education and his job, which he needed to support himself, because he felt his parents had their hands full supporting the family, in particular catering to his two sisters' needs. His schedule didn't allow him any time to wash and iron his school clothes, and even his regular clothes, which he would put in the cleaner each week.

Later, at the mature age of fifteen, he wanted to buy a car; but he was too young for credit and too young to drive. And he didn't have enough money to buy one. Robert's father knew he was a hard worker and was saving his money, so he decided to make Robert a proposition. He told Robert he would co-sign for the car, if Robert would pay him to do so.

Without hesitation, Robert agreed to pay his father to co-sign for him for the car. His mother was very angry and frustrated, shaming his father for even making such a proposition. She said, "He's your son, and you're going to charge him for you to co-sign for him?"

His father was so ashamed, but he did not keep to their arrangement for Robert to pay him, leaving Robert with a two-car note to pay at the age of fifteen. His father borrowed the down payment from Sun Finance, and then signed up with the General Motors Acceptance Corporation (GMAC) to finance the car. Which meant Robert had to pay Sun Finance for the down payment and GMAC for the car's financing.

What was even more devastating was that Robert was too young to get a driver's license, and he didn't know how to drive. Robert didn't want the car for himself; he wanted it for his mother. It made him happy to think that he could do something for his mother, like get her a car that would make it easier for her to get to and from work. Yes, he had been robbed of his childhood, made to assume the responsibilities of an adult while still in a kid's body; but getting a car for his mother was something he wanted to do.

Going to school and working, he never was one day late in paying both his car notes, because he didn't want it to go back to his father. In fact, his parents hardly saw him; because he was too busy trying to meet his obligations. His home was only a place where he laid his head for very little sleep.

One day, after he had reported to work, his supervisor informed him he was being laid off. Robert was very disturbed; he didn't know how to tell his mother and his father that he no longer had a job. His first day of being out of a job, Robert isolated himself, hiding under his bed after school, staying quiet as a mouse, not even going to the bathroom until his shift was over, to keep his parents from finding out what happened. The next day, his job called him back, and his parents never knew that he had gotten laid off.

He was so overwhelmed to be back at work, knowing he wouldn't be able to face his father if he had lost his job for good. A short time later, he noticed how his mother would isolate herself out on the back porch, sitting on the steps in the darkness, crying. He knew things with his parents weren't going as well, but to see his mother crying was really tearing him apart. His mother would never tell him why she was crying; she would just smile and tell him in her soft-spoken voice, "I'm all right." Her smile couldn't hide the tears that were running down her face. He felt as though he knew her pain; and seeing his mother cry, he cried with her inside.

Yet even as she was going through her silent storm, her love for her kids would shine through with the warmth of her smile. Robert and his sisters were afraid of their father, and so was their mother. Their father had the voice of a giant, and no one in the household was allowed to use the phone. When their mother did talk on the phone, it was only when he wasn't around. As soon as she would see him driving up the driveway, she would immediately hang up the phone. And when he entered the house, you could hear a pin drop.

Their father was very strict and very firm in his beliefs. Not once did they chuckle over what he said or did, or let him know in any way that they disagreed with his beliefs.

At times, they would find themselves running out of the back door when he got hostile and started yelling at them at the top of his voice.

Everyone would quickly get out of his way. Even when they were on the move, they were so afraid; all he had to say was "Halt," and they would freeze in their tracks. Robert's mother was trapped in a marriage filled with fear; she was a prisoner in her own home. But she and her kids knew they had nowhere to go.

Julie, the youngest, got pregnant at a very early age being a teenager and married her baby's father—a guy named Lester. Julie was their father's favorite, and it hurt him when she got pregnant. He wanted Julie to say Lester had raped her, but deep down, he knew rape wasn't the case.

Their father didn't like Lester; he didn't want Julie to see him or have anything to do with him. Anyone in the household having a phone conversation with someone, male or female, was totally out of the question as far as their father was concerned. He would always say his phone was for business only; therefore, he was the only one in the household who could use the phone.

After Julie was married, she moved out to live with her husband, leaving Robert and Sally and their mother. Robert wondered if getting pregnant and married was Julie's way of escaping from under their father's roof.

Robert could remember that as a child, he wanted to be in law enforcement, because he couldn't stand the thought of anyone taking anything from him. He attended Franklin Junior High School in his sophomore year, where he was accused of committing a crime that he had no knowledge of. One day he was called into the principal's office, where two police officers were waiting to question him, in the presence of a witness—the supposed victim, who accused Robert of stabbing him with a knife.

The witness identified Robert with no doubt as the person who had stabbed him. Robert had a friend named Russell, and the witness said that after Robert had stabbed him, he said, "Come on, Russell." The witness was so convincing he almost convinced Robert that he had really committed the crime.

The witness described Robert from head to toe. Robert just knew he was getting ready to pay for a crime he didn't commit and had no knowledge of. In fact, he couldn't recall ever seeing his accuser before in his life, and he wondered what his accuser motive was for setting him up.

With the witness's description, the police officers had enough evidence to take Robert into custody.

The charge was aggravated assault with a weapon and attempted murder. Robert was so shocked about the whole ordeal he was speechless. He knew he was going to jail. Robert snapped out of his daze and started to defend himself. He told the police officer to ask their witness what day and time the stabbing occurred.

The victim gave the date and time, and Robert quickly pointed out that he was at work when the crime was committed.

The police officer had the principal call Robert's job to establish the time that he punched in and out on the date the witness mentioned. The officer was considerate enough to tell the principal not to let Robert's employer know what the matter was, because he didn't want Robert to lose his job if he was innocent. Robert's boss's answer cleared him from the crime.

The police looked at their witness and said it was impossible for Robert to have committed the crime because he was at work at the time of the stabbing. The so-called victim broke down in tears crying, because he knew he had just been caught in a lie, and an innocent person could have been sent to jail for a crime he didn't commit. Robert just sat there quietly as his mind drifted. He was never the type to be quick to judge anyone until he had walked a mile in their shoes. What mattered more to him now was that his innocence had been proven.

And in the back of Robert's mind, he wondered how many more like him were there, only they had not been so lucky—incarcerated, either for a specific number of years or for life, or even sentenced to death for something they didn't commit or knew anything about. He shook his head as his mind drifted. You had to be a victim to know how it felt to be accused of something you did not commit. And with no doubt, he knew many more people who were incarcerated. They were the real victims, paying the price for something they didn't do.

After Julie had left, Robert got exhausted with the way his father was treating his mother. Every night he would come home and yell at her for no apparent reason. It was as though he was forcing her to leave. Robert had made up in his mind. Enough was enough.

Again, he found his mother sitting in the darkness out on the back porch trying to hide her tears. He was very surprised when she told him she wanted to leave but just did not have the money to do so. But Robert had always known his mother was very miserable, and now, finally, she was ready to leave. She said she wanted to go to Chicago.

He gazed at her and felt deep sadness he didn't want his mother to leave. But with no hesitation, he asked her how much money she needed to leave. He loved her too much to let her stay and watch her just sitting in the darkness—hiding her tears, camouflaging her pain.

He told his mother, "I'll give you the money you need to pay your fare, and money you need to travel."

On the day she was to leave, she waited until his father had left for work. She did not even leave him a note. Robert suddenly felt so much weight on his shoulders.

A short time after, Sally ended up leaving New Orleans to go back to Mississippi to finish school, and she eventually married a guy named Joseph, leaving Robert alone with his father. Robert felt trapped being in a home that he hated, hating even more the fact that even though there was just him and his father now, they did not have any relationship. There was no communication between them whatsoever; they might as well have been total strangers.

Still, it was the only home Robert knew. When he was seventeen, he made an attempt to join the marines to get away from home, where he was now left only with memories of his mother and his two sisters.

The Vietnam War was going on at the time, and so many American soldiers were getting killed each day. The war was a bloodbath. Robert went to the recruiting office to sign up, saying he wanted to be shipped out as soon as possible. Since he was a minor, the recruiting officer gave him some papers for his father to sign. The marines needed his parents' signature to let him join, and Robert was his parents' only son.

Robert brought the papers home and asked his father to sign them, simply saying he wanted to join the military.

His father looked at him and replied, "If you think I'm going to sign these papers for you to get yourself killed, you are crazy."

That was his first attempt to escape from a house he wasn't happy in. His next step was marriage. He had a girlfriend, Jessica, whom he loved very much; and all that was on his mind was getting her pregnant, which would give him an excuse to marry her, escaping a house he now used only for sleeping.

CHAPTER 3

Robert's First Wife and
The Skeletons in His Closet

S HORTLY AFTER ROBERT'S GIRLFRIEND BECAME pregnant, he asked
her parents for their permission to marry her. He was very nervous
and scared, with no anticipation of things going his way. He never
could forget about going in her parents' bedroom, shaking like a leaf, and
telling them their daughter was pregnant. He was very surprised by their
response; they seemed pleased, as though he was doing them a favor. He
chuckled, thinking he could have charged them a fee for taking her off
their hands.

Robert stood there quietly. Then Jessica's parents asked him, had they
set a date for the wedding? So he gave her parents a date; he had very little

time to plan. He wanted to do it quick, so Jessica's mother didn't hesitate starting to make plans for the wedding. Robert went out and bought a new suit—in fact, his only suit. Little did Jessica's parents know that Robert didn't tell his father anything at all about his wedding until a day before.

Robert ended up dropping out of school and working for a place called Dixie Tomatoes. At seventeen, he looked very mature for his age. He lied on his job application and put down his age at twenty-one. And his girlfriend continued her schooling during her pregnancy.

The wedding date was approaching, and Robert knew he had to tell his father something. Trusting his instincts, he approached his father to tell him. His father knew Robert was serious because he had never approached him in such of a manner before. In the moment of silence, his father blindly reached in back of him for a chair to sit down, and then was all ears to Robert's news, not interrupting him at all. Robert guessed his father was saying to himself, *Oh Lord, here we go again.*

Robert grew very nervous again, but he didn't hesitate in telling his father his girlfriend was pregnant, and that he wanted to marry her and the wedding was only a day away. His father was very calm and accepted the fact Robert wanted to stand up on his own two feet and face his responsibilities. In fact, he seemed very happy and gave his son his blessing.

Robert couldn't help thinking about a guy who lived down the street whom Jessica liked. His name was Adam.

Robert could tell just by the expression on her face every time Adam would drive by her house and wave at her that maybe she had a crush on him. He could see it in her smile when he was near, but still he remained silent. He needed this marriage to escape from the place he called home.

The wedding was set for July 15, 1972. Robert felt that he wasn't a cub anymore but a full-grown bear. He thought he had it all together, but not even once did he give a thought to where he and Jessica were going to live after the wedding.

His attempt to join the marines and get married to escape from his father still brought him to the same room. The only difference was that now he wasn't alone. Now he had a wife. He loved his wife beyond measure and had her best interest at heart. During Jessica's pregnancy, she was always sick, so he would always come home after work and cook and clean for her. His father got very angry because she had been home all day but there was no meal. He made sure to express his disapproval.

Although he explained to his father how sick Jessica was, it didn't make a difference, and it didn't help his craving for food. Even as a child, Robert had always respected his father, and he thought it was best for him to move. The very next day, he and Jessica moved into a one-bedroom duplex. And he managed to get some furniture on credit. And at the time, his hourly rate on his job was about eighty cents.

Robert did a lot of overtime work to be able to provide for their needs. He had become a workaholic, and the only thing he knew to do even as a child was work. It didn't take him long to discover it wasn't easy being the man of the house, not to mention being a father, as he would soon find out.

Although he was working long hours, he would never have enough money for his lunch, but he made sure Jessica had food to eat while he was at work. He was more than any woman could want in a man and a husband. However, after Jessica started feeling better, she remained in the same state. She did nothing, which made Robert feel that she did really appreciate their marriage, and him.

He thought at first that her sickness was hindering her from doing her household chores; and nevertheless, she wasn't a good cook, and neither was she a good housekeeper. After he had worked long hours and came home exhausted, Robert thought she would at least prepare him a sandwich for dinner, to show a little effort, but even that was asking too much.

Jessica had so many conflicting emotions. Robert felt his marriage was falling apart at a very early stage, and he was very concerned, because he wanted his wife to have more emotional investment in the marriage and show her love for him. He took his marriage vows very seriously and believed marriage was forever.

Instead, things got so critical that once, he just found himself shaking and trembling at work. His hands were shaking. His subconscious had been telling him how bad his marriage was, and now the realization was starting to affect him. He loved her just that much.

She showed no interest at all in their relationship, in their marriage. He felt she had become totally heartless despite knowing she had a husband who loved her. As far as she was concerned, her marriage license was just a piece of paper, and him leaving her was the least of her worries.

On one particular day, he had worked long hours and was very tired and just wanted to go home and have dinner and relax. When he arrived home, though, he saw that Jessica, as usual, had not prepared any dinner, with no explanation; instead, she asked him to take her to her parents' house. Wanting only to please her, Robert did as she asked without hesitation. On the way there, she told him she wanted to go to a baby shower one of her friends was having. He told her he was tired and had to get up early for work the next morning.

She said she wasn't going to the party until after she had gotten around by her parents. And then all hell broke loose. She got very arrogant. She ridiculed him in front of her parents, saying she didn't care what Robert said; she was going to the baby shower. She made Robert feel very small and embarrassed in front of her parents. She had taken things to the extreme, to the point where only what she wanted mattered. For some reason, she was a totally a different person around her relatives; she reminded him of a werewolf that changed with the moon.

Her actions were totally unpredictable and untamed. For some reason, she wanted her relatives to think she was in control of their marriage. She didn't realize how bad she had hurt him in front of her parents, but still, he stayed at her parents', waiting till she returned from the baby shower. There was no doubt she didn't want a husband but, rather, a puppet on a string.

The more love he showed her, the more she thought she was in control. Robert got so depressed and needed a friend to talk to; he could no longer try to keep his frustration bottled up within. One day at work, he spent his lunch hour with a girl called Teresa, and they would become the best of friends.

Teresa seemed to feel his pain and understand his problems and what he was going through. And talking to her about his problems was his way of getting some release after keeping so much bottled up within him. He felt like an overloaded fuse that was getting ready to blow, not knowing which way to go. Teresa was so much more mature in age than Robert.

In fact, Teresa was about twenty-six, and Robert was only seventeen. Robert never told Teresa his true age. Teresa was a very attractive lady, with a beautiful figure that really turned Robert on, resurrecting his desire for a woman. He did not know his attraction to her would lead to him being unfaithful to his wife. Her body left him starving, lusting after her with just a glance at her. His male ego applauded him and urged him on with heated passion for her. Teresa seemed to be a perfect woman in every way.

Robert had always thought that because of his religious beliefs, his first wife would always be his wife. He believed in his vows. But as the days went by, he found himself falling in love with Teresa, and he knew she was falling in love with him too. He felt he was hanging from a cliff and was losing his grip. Teresa had a boyfriend at the time, but she herself was in a bad relationship; and before Robert knew it, one thing led to the next.

He found himself in bed with another woman. He felt that he had betrayed his wife, and this bothered him a lot. Cheating and lying went hand in hand. You couldn't do one without doing the other. Lying was a road with no end.

Robert knew he would always have to cover the first lie with another lie, the second lie with a third, and so on. Robert felt he had violated his marriage and his vows the first time, and he felt hurt; but the more he did it, the easier it got each time. After a while, he wondered where his conscience was, and his guilt had turned into numbness, for the way his wife had treated him.

Teresa gave Robert all the attention he wanted and acted as though she really did care about him and was concerned about his well-being. She gave him the attention he wasn't getting at home, and he gave her the attention her boyfriend wasn't giving her. Finally, Teresa separated from her boyfriend.

Robert found himself pulling back from her after she had left her boyfriend; he couldn't promise her a commitment because of his marriage, and he was afraid she would ask him to leave his wife. Things seemed to be going very well for him, until Teresa informed him she was pregnant. After hearing what she had said, Robert thought about his wife. What if she found out about Teresa and her pregnancy?

To Robert, this was really a nightmare. And he felt drained from head to toe. He never wanted any other kids outside of his marriage.

He had no idea what the outcome of this would be, but Jessica still stayed in the same mode, not showing any interest in him and his well-being. In his mind, Robert accepted the fact of Teresa's pregnancy, but this still didn't change the fact that he was living a double life. He could only hope no one would ever find out. He was feeling more depressed than ever.

His wife expecting to have his baby as well devastated Robert; the skeleton in his closet was going to reveal itself sooner or later. But as time went on, he tried to distance himself from Teresa. A short time later, Teresa gave birth to a baby boy.

Throughout her pregnancy, Teresa had always thought the baby was Robert's, but it was later determined that the baby was her ex-boyfriend's. She had conceived before leaving him.

Robert felt as though the whole world had been lifted off his shoulder. He knew Teresa wasn't trying to deceive him; actually, she didn't know for sure who the father of her baby was, because during this time, she was still sleeping with both men.

Meanwhile, Jessica had some complications during her pregnancy, and the doctor had to deliver the baby earlier because her life and the baby's were in danger. Her blood pressure was too high. Being that this was his first child, Robert was very worried. He prayed for his wife and his baby; he didn't want to lose either one of them.

Finally, the doctor had to perform a Cesarean. The baby was a girl, and born premature. Robert was very proud of her. At this point, he wanted to be the best father and husband both of them could ever ask for.

Jessica and the baby eventually came home from the hospital; her recovery was remarkable. Robert was a proud father, showering his baby daughter with so much of love and affection. There was no doubt he was spoiling her. Meanwhile, Jessica was a wonderful mother, but she was ignoring her obligations as a wife to him.

The only thing they had in common was sex, and she drew the line beyond that. She withheld the love and affection for which he thirsted.

Robert would brace himself coming home to a dirty house after a long and hard day at work. He would cook and sweep and mop the floors. Nothing about Jessica had changed; she remained lazy, sitting around doing nothing; and when she would sweep the floor, she would sweep the trash into a corner and leave it there.

And every chance she got, she would be rude to him and make him look bad in front of her relatives; but still Robert felt she was his wife and was hoping for their relationship to get better. But the truth was that she wasn't making any effort to change. She gave him the impression she saw him as her robot. He could take it or leave it; it didn't matter to her one way or the other.

And again, one thing led to the next; and he and Teresa got very intimate with each other again. He started seeing her on a regular basis. She wanted him to leave his wife, but he would feel less than a man if he did so.

Robert would tell her, "If I leave my wife for you, how do you know I wouldn't leave you for someone else?" He knew he would never leave his wife for another woman, no matter what. He felt he never could live with himself if he did so.

Teresa was willing to accept Robert as he was. Where you found Robert, you found Teresa. They grew very close in all the time they shared together every day at work. They would always isolate themselves from others. They would make love at work, and his emotions overwhelmed him. He was blinded and crippled by his freakish feelings for her. His mind drifted. It was easy finding fault in his wife, hiding the fault within himself, putting the blame on someone else. It was just human nature.

As time went on, Teresa became pregnant again; but this time, she was pregnant by Robert. Around the same time, Jessica was pregnant as well. As with before, Robert regretted Teresa's pregnancy. He didn't believe he had let his emotion get in the way, allowing this to happen. He was becoming more of a candidate for a divorce if his wife found out about Teresa.

Robert found himself angry with Teresa for letting this happen, but not once did he question himself why he didn't use some form of protection. He was only eighteen years old at the time. He tried to distance himself from Teresa, hoping the nightmare would just go away.

Young and foolish, Robert refused to accept the responsibility of being the father of Teresa's baby, hoping her pregnancy would go away. But because they worked together, he saw her every day, and it seemed as though she was getting bigger and bigger each day.

Even after all that Robert did, Teresa still treated him the same way. She had a heart of gold, and he had never seen her angry or upset about anything.

She worked up to the time when she had to go on maternity leave, and he was glad, because seeing her was a reminder that he had gotten another woman pregnant. He stayed out of contact with her until she had the baby. Jessica, his churchgoing wife, had totally blinded him despite her behavior, driven by the coldness of her heart.

The Bible said cleanliness was to next to godliness, and he couldn't believe the way she kept their home. Still sweeping trash into a corner and leaving it there. The only time he felt she did care a little was when he was taken ill. She waited on him hand and foot. He wondered if this was her way of saying, *I need you to get better for you to get back to work.*

And even then, he couldn't help but wonder if she didn't want to cut off the hand that was feeding her. Robert really felt close to his daughter. Yes, she was a daddy's girl, and even much so, his daughter gave him more than a reason to stay with his family.

Robert pampered Jessica during her second pregnancy; he was concerned about her well-being because he remembered the complications from her first. Although there had not been any complications during the pregnancy, she still ended up giving birth through the Cesarean method. This time they had a beautiful baby girl, whom they named Sherry. Sherry was Robert's heart also.

A few months before, Teresa had given birth to a baby boy, whom she named Anthony. The baby had many of Robert's features.

Still, Robert had some doubts in his mind as to whether the baby was really his.

Because the baby had a lot of his features, Robert wanted even more so to deny that the baby was his. After a few months, Jessica got a job, and Robert would stay with the kids on his off day while she was at work. One day, he left their younger daughter with his sister because he had to go take care of some business.

When Jessica heard about him leaving their daughter with his sister, she was frustrated and told her parents. Her father informed Robert he shouldn't leave his kids with just anyone.

Robert got so angry he lashed out: "What do you mean? My sister is not just anyone?" It was one of Jessica's tactics—trying to make him look small in front of her relatives.

Robert didn't hesitate to leave her parents' home. He was hurt by what was said.

Living a double life—being married with two kids and another outside his marriage—was very hard. One woman was treating him as though she really did care, and the other one was just going through the motions. The way his wife was treating him around her relatives was really obnoxious, and he hated it.

No matter how much she embarrassed him, it never crossed his mind to divorce her. In his mind, marriage was forever and no matter what, he would never leave her, even more so now for the kids' sake.

It was as though there was a cancer inside of him eating him up every time he would think about Teresa and their baby. He was so confused; he did not know how to deal with his wife and Teresa. He loved his wife to the point where he was always feeling restless because of her lack of love for him. He felt that there was no love in his marriage, no matter how much he gave and how much he was willing to give still. He was turning into a total wreck, because what she was showing him gave him very little hope for their marriage.

As always, Teresa was there to listen. She seemed to be there for him and was willing to give him what he couldn't find in his wife. Although he had turned his back on Teresa during her pregnancy, she forgave him, never once mentioning how bad he had treated her when she needed him the most. Teresa's timing was everything; she listened when he felt so depressed over his wife. She would listen when he had so much trapped inside. She had passion for him when he felt no one really cared.

Robert knew without a doubt that Teresa was a better woman than his wife because of what she gave him and how secure she made him feel. Teresa would kiss and hug him when he needed it the most, but never would he have thought that her caring about him would lead to another pregnancy.

Teresa's second pregnancy made Robert even more depressed. It was like quicksand: the more he wiggled, the more he sank. But even worse, his wife was pregnant again. Deep down, he couldn't help but wonder if this was Teresa's way of trapping him. He felt angry and distanced himself from her. In the back of his mind, he had to wonder if she was really pregnant by him or by someone else. He felt the darkness of his conscience.

Robert was in total denial. He knew it was wrong to have kids outside of his marriage—and even worse was not being sure if she was really pregnant by him.

A short time after, he decided to move to Pascagoula, Mississippi, leaving his wife behind. The plan was for him to send for her when he found a job, but he missed her so that he sent for her before then. A very short time upon her arrival, he found a job at a shipyard called Ingalls Shipbuilding. Being away from New Orleans made him feel as though he was starting his life all over. There was nothing to remind him of what he had left behind in New Orleans, not even Teresa.

He wanted to give his marriage a new beginning. He wanted a good relationship with his wife, because he really did love her. Jessica never did seem hooked on material things. In fact, nothing seemed to excite her. She lived for the day only, and tomorrow didn't matter.

Away from her family, her attitude was totally different. In fact, he felt their relationship was headed for a new beginning. A short time later, Jessica found a job in a hospital in Pascagoula. Things were really looking up. They had their next baby, a boy, in Pascagoula. They named him Robert the IV.

After being away from New Orleans for a while, Robert found out Teresa had a baby boy around the same time Jessica gave birth again, and a new boyfriend as well. At that point, right after he had found out about her boyfriend, he lost all interest in her. Even more so, he was in total denial of being the father of her kid. When he saw the baby for the first time, he realized that his son by his wife and Teresa's baby could have passed for twins. One was a little darker-skinned than the other, but he could tell they were brothers.

He was even more disturbed by the fact that he knew he was the father of Teresa's baby. Even more so, not being able to tell anyone about his kids and his encounter with Teresa troubled him a lot. He was hoping his wife would never find out, because it would hurt her. He wondered what image she would have of him if she did find out about his kids with another woman. He knew this would generate conflicting emotions.

He felt ashamed of his behavior because he always wanted to be a perfect husband to his wife and a perfect father to his kids, but to hold that title was only in his imagination now.

Robert had lost all feelings for Teresa, especially when he found out she had another boyfriend. Deep down, he knew the way he had treated her was more than fair, when he had left and gone on with his life.

Robert had visited New Orleans and then left everything behind him when he went back to Pascagoula, even Teresa and their kids. They would only live in the shadows of his mind.

Later, when he did try to contact her, he found out she had kept her number private, so he now did not know her whereabouts and the kids'. He lived with many regrets over never knowing the whereabouts of his kids. He had been so young and immature, and now he regretted not being in his kids' lives, living in the shadows of his past, and his kids not really knowing their father.

In Pascagoula, things were looking up. He went from a chipper to a cable puller to a forklift operator, and it was really beginning to pay off. He was bringing home over $600 a week, and in 1975, that was very good money. He would work a lot of overtime hours, and overtime was unlimited. In fact, he was a workaholic. Working was his way of keeping his mind off things.

Robert always wanted his wife and kids to have the best, always wanting to improve their well-being and their living conditions. They were living in an apartment in Gautier, Mississippi. He wanted so much more for his kids and his wife, so he decided to buy a house.

Robert started looking at different houses with different realties for the perfect home for his family. One house, which was a fairly newly constructed home, he loved very much, and Jessica liked it as well. He put down some honest money on the house and then waited for approval.

He was very excited about putting his family in a lovely home. A short time later, he was informed that he had been approved for the house, and he was very excited. He wanted only ten years' mortgage instead of thirty years. He had an idea of paying the house off in ten years, He wanted to double his mortgage each month and work down the principal each month.

When he approached his wife with his ideas, all he asked of her for the next ten years was that she take care of the kids and herself, because she was working too. He told her he would still pay the car note and the utility bills. All he needed from her was for her to buy clothes for the kids and shop for groceries, and he would take care of the rest each month. When he told her of his idea, she got totally upset and very arrogant. Undoubtedly, she didn't like his idea.

She said, "If you do that with your money, I'll stop working." She wasn't going to help Robert.

He was so upset with her that he didn't buy the house. He tried again a second time, but her attitude was still the same. After that, he gave up trying to purchase a home she didn't appreciate. She was never interested in material things, which he did.

She lived one day at a time, just going through the motions. At times, he couldn't help wondering if she had someone else in her life. She had gotten back in the same mode as before. She seemed to want nothing more and nothing less.

He could remember how on one occasion, his wife had made a comment about how cute one of his friends was, and he couldn't help wondering, did he really know the woman he had married? The years they had been married, he couldn't remember her even once commenting on his appearance or how handsome he was.

He thought he could trust her because she was a churchgoing woman with religious beliefs, but in his mind, there was always a question mark. But he was also in total denial, so he never imagined her not being faithful. Later, he decided he was going back to New Orleans after living in Pascagoula for about four years. He found a job in New Orleans as a deputy sheriff. Being in law enforcement had always been his desire, even as a child. Just a few days later, he was called to take the examination to become a deputy sheriff.

Upon passing all his examinations, he was later hired as a deputy sheriff—a job he really did like.

He was very good at his job, and his superiors were impressed by his performance. He worked twelve hours a day and loved what he was doing. And had very little time to focus on his marriage, although he loved his kids. Jessica stayed home when she wasn't at work or at church. And she didn't see cleaning the house as her main responsibility, and little did she know it was really turning Robert off.

She was the worst housekeeper he had ever seen. The house was always dirty; if it was a garden, he could plant seeds and grow vegetables inside the house with a little bit of sunlight and water. She was always eager to go to church, not letting anything stand in her way. The church she attended was the same one she attended as a child, and the same one where he met her.

The pastor of the church had a son, who was approximately Jessica's age and a preacher as well. Never did Robert think she had any interest in him, or he in her. But once in a while, his name would come up. Never once did he feel he was in a predicament, nor did he even think about his wife having an affair with a preacher.

She was always going to church or choir rehearsal, and they had nothing in common but their kids. What was most astonishing was how she never seemed to want them to spend time together. She went to church, and he went out to bars.

What was more fascinating was how both of them seemed as though they were contended to go their separate ways. The stimulus in his marriage just wasn't there, and nothing seemed to magnify the vows they made to each other. He was really close to his kids; in fact, their oldest daughter was surely a daddy's girl.

As far as Robert was concerned, his marriage was forever, and he never thought he would see the day when his wife would have an affair with another man. His religious belief would never let him marry another woman as long as his wife was still living. He believed in God, and he would heed the Word of God and honor his marriage vows.

One day, while they were at home enjoying each other's company for once, he felt there might be hope for their marriage after all. But out of nowhere, Jessica's sister Jane came over; and all at once, his wife's whole attitude changed, and she got very belligerent with him. She said, "You can go to hell." Robert thought she was trying to prove a point to her sister.

Her behavior left no room for an explanation. Robert remained silent and just got in his car and left. After driving two blocks, it hit him with anger. And he put the car in reverse and backed up and drove all the way back home, He entered the house and said to his wife, "What did you say?"

She was in such outrage her sister thought Robert had mistreated her. Jessica's sister, a very heavyset woman, had words to say to him about her sister, and he replied, "You big polar bear, this does not concern you."

Jessica started packing her clothes, and Robert didn't know why she was in such outrage, and what had happened. He was totally speechless, and couldn't comprehend what was going on, other than she was making him look small in front of her sister.

He waited until she was through packing her things, and she told him in the presence of her sister, "When you start seeing things my way, you can come and get me."

Again, just that statement alone didn't make any sense at all. He told her, "You will be waiting a long time."

Taking his kids with her was the most hurtful thing she had done to him. He struggled with himself not having his kids home, and he was hoping maybe there was a possibility she would bring them home. At first, he remained neutral and didn't make any attempt to fix the situation because of the way she left.

And deep down, he was missing his wife as well; but he was still angry and had too much pride to go get her after what she had said to him in front of her sister. She absolutely had no idea how she had separated him from the people he loved most—his kids.

Coming home and not seeing his kids became very unbearable for Robert. He went by Jessica's sister's house, and he made some attempt to pamper her, hoping she would come home; but he found her antipathy toward putting in any effort unpleasant. She seemed untouchable, with no feelings at all.

In the years they were married, they never had a fight or a big argument. Robert couldn't help but wonder what the real reason was for her abandoning her marriage all of a sudden. Still, he had no doubt in his mind: she was involved with another man. It was easy for him to fantasize of the kind of marriage he wanted, but hard for him to accept the way things really were.

From Jessica's reaction, she had undoubtedly embraced her notions and had burdened their marriage with no impression of returning home. Her transformed mind was untouchable, and her thoughts were unstoppable, and she had a very narrow mind. From her expression, it seemed as though she had planned this—leaving him with no say-so. She was totally uncontrollable. He made it very clear how much he loved his kids and how he missed them dearly. Nevertheless, she seemed willing to jeopardize their marriage and had no problem separating him from his kids.

Robert felt once again that she wanted to be in control, and this was her opportunity to establish her escape and to achieve her goals, which were inspired by her religious beliefs. Frustrated, Robert decided to follow his instincts to be firm, leaving her where she wanted to be and taking his kids. He took his oldest daughter and attempted to get her in the car.

And his oldest child, Sandra, was trapped between situations she had no knowledge of. Jessica called the police to stop him from taking the kids.

Upon the police's arrival, they looked inside Robert's vehicle and saw his uniform shirt. One of the officers said, "Let me talk to you as another law enforcement officer."

Under the circumstances, Robert knew it was best not to be argumentative, and it wasn't in his best interest that he tried to take the kids the way he did.

CHAPTER 4

Jessica and Abby

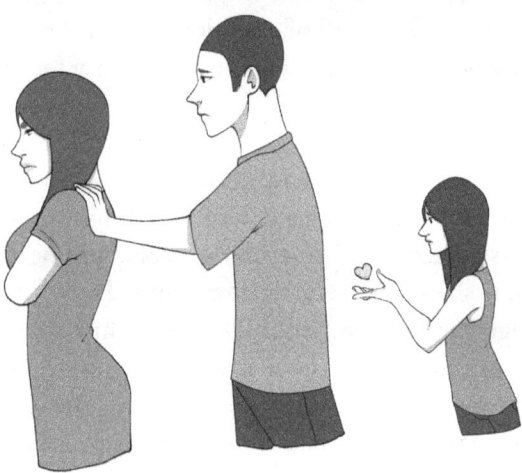

S LOWLY BUT SURELY, ROBERT KNEW his marriage was crumbling, just by his wife's actions. He knew it wasn't just his imagination; Jessica was ready to move forward in a different direction. Finally, she admitted to having an affair with her pastor's son.

Robert chuckled, unable to understand her behavior: having an affair and being a saint in the church and a hypocrite in the bedroom.

Needless to say, it seemed as though the whole atmosphere around him had changed. Everything seemed to be dramatized. He shuddered just thinking about his wife in bed with another man—and a preacher at that. He felt she had anticipated such an act, which was just irresponsible. But still, he was being very mature and accepted the fact, and was willing to forgive her and hold his tongue because of his guilt from having an affair with Teresa, which she never knew about. Robert's mind drifted with a thought: He had an affair and two kids outside of his marriage, and Jessica was having an affair with a preacher in the course of their marriage as well. Whose sin was greater? Through their transgressions, no sin outweighed the other, no matter how larger or how small. A sin was a sin. Satan had marked his territory and revealed himself in them both.

In Robert's mind, his marriage vows were unconditional, and he wanted to do the proper thing of starting a new life with his family. Still, Jessica had a bizarre way of showing her interest in putting the family back together. Her lover approached Robert with guidance to remind him of his obligations, in reference to his kids, and Robert felt as though he was an overloaded circuit. He punched the preacher in the face, and his action was unmerciful. The preacher ran, shielding himself behind Jessica, as though he had died and gone to hell. Robert's anger left him in a uproar disgracing Jessica more than what she deserved because he was less than being perfect himself. A short time later, Robert made friends with Nick, who had a cousin from Jackson, Mississippi, named Abby; and she came to New Orleans to get away from a relationship. In fact, the guy she was involved with brought her there. Robert listened to Abby's boy friend talk about her; he was very precise and honest, nodded his head used hand gestures to reply. She is a good woman, and he was going to miss her leaving her in New Orleans.

Robert admired Abby. At this point, he was finding it intolerable putting up with his wife's behavior. He just couldn't deal with her twisted mind and her sarcastic attitude. Abby was very attractive and sexy, but her use of marijuana made him uncertain about having a relationship with her.

On one occasion, he had just gotten off duty when he observed her in her car smoking marijuana with a friend. He opened the car door, interrupting her, and put his handcuffs around her wrists and informed her she was under arrest.

Her eyes rolled to the back of her head, and he couldn't help from laughing. It was so funny. He was laughing while he was taking the handcuffs from around her wrists. She jumped out of the car and hopped up and down, as though she was going to piss on herself scared to death, running with her big purse, not looking back, not even once. Whatever her celebration was getting high, it was surely over.

She was so frightened she totally forgot Nick had introduced her to him. She ran straight to Nick, asking him who Robert was. Her astonishment left her witless. He swiftly tried to perk her up after he had left a bad taste in her mouth. She was angry and refused to carry on a conversation. Her frustration overpowered his impulse to apologize to her. She was frowning and murmuring under her breath, "I don't play like that. I don't play with policemen."

Robert just chuckled, not pushing her button any farther. To him, she was very attractive and desirable and was a sex symbol. She was a new girl on the block, and a lot of the guys were after her. Everything about her was sexy, even her walk. He knew his chances with her would be nonexistent because he had dated her first cousin for a short period, which eventually ended after he walked in on her cousin with another man.

And after his invasion of her "privacy," her cousin showed a dislike toward him, as though she was angry that he had caught her with another man. He thought her action was pitiful, being angry at him after he found out about her affair with another man. Abby was living with Nick when Robert found himself making Nick home's his first stop after work before going home. Nick had another friend by the name of James, who was a friend of Robert's as well.

It was just unfortunate that Robert and James had the same interest at heart, and that was Abby. However, Abby and James had more in common than Robert did with Abby, because they were both marijuana users. Also, there were Albert, Willie, Tom, and a guy who called himself Shot. And there were many other guys who were after Abby. They all had her on their agenda. She was showered with attention.

Robert desired Abby, even if it was just for one night; but his mind was still on his wife. Abby knew he had had an affair with her cousin. Deep down he knew her cousin and her family would ridicule Abby if she dated him. Slowly but surely, she began to show a little attraction toward him.

More and more each night, Robert found himself in the nightclubs where Nick was working as a disc jockey. Abby would be there, surrounded by a lot of guys who admired her. And night after night, the same guys surrounded Abby.

Robert felt as though he was in competition with so many others who desired her. Still, he kept his feelings pretty well hidden, even though his frustration made him feel more and more that he was competing with the guys who constantly surrounded her, as though she was the only woman in town.

Robert decided to walk out of the club, feeling very frustrated. His emotions crumbled, and he was fed up with Abby and her other friends. He felt it was time for him to bow out, so he decided to get out of the race. He left the club and went home. About fifteen minutes later, he heard a knock at his door. He replied, who is it, she replied, it's me, Abby.

He was in shock, not knowing how she got there, because she had no car. When he asked her, she replied, "I had James drop me off."

Robert was shocked, knowing James was after her too. From that point on, he knew chasing after her was over; slowly but surely, their relationship was getting deeper.

Abby's confused mind left her speechless because Robert had had a relationship with her cousin, and that disturbed her. Little did she know what really happened. Abby's disapproval with his relationship with her cousin existed for a moment, but then her thoughts were interrupted by her heated passion to make love to him.

More and more each day, Robert was falling in love with Abby, and Abby was falling in love with him. In her own bizarre way, she felt she had to ask for her cousin's permission before entering into a deeper relationship with him. Robert felt he owed her cousin no explanation, but Abby had to ask in her own sophisticated way in order to clear her conscience.

After Abby had gone to her cousin to tell her about her interest in Robert, her cousin, in her twisted mind, gave her approval by mouth, but her heart was farther away. She felt Abby was being disloyal, and having a relationship with Robert was unacceptable in her mind. Abby's cousin's whole attitude changed like a whirlwind toward Abby, leaving a whiplash between the two of them, who were at one time like sisters.

Robert was disturbed by Abby's cousin's attitude, and he did not know whether or not he and Abby would ever have a future together, but still, it would leave such a flaw in Abby's life with her cousin. Robert still hadn't recovered from his wife's betrayal, and he missed his kids dearly. He had to wonder if his feelings for his wife would ever diminish.

Abby's actions started to prevail over Robert. She made sure to be with him every chance she got; and slowly but surely, Robert started to lose his feelings for his wife.

Robert knew Abby had fallen in love with him, and him going back to his wife would really hurt Abby after what they had been through.

Besides, Robert knew his wife's mind was still scrambled over her lover, and that she was incapable of making a decision between the two of them. And for that reason, he decided to go on with his life and gave in to his desire to share his life with Abby. He moved out of the house and into a place in New Orleans called New Orleans East.

Things with him and Abby were starting to move rather fast. In a matter of days, Abby had more clothes in the closet than Robert did. She had moved in with no doubt. Then Abby and Robert's ex-wife and her sister ended up spending a night together due to a threat of hurricane. Jessica and the kids lived in a high-risk area, so Abby agreed to let them stay over for their safety. And being a deputy sheriff, Robert had to work the night shift, but his mind was on Abby, and how remarkable her attitude was toward his ex-wife and his kids.

Thank God, the hurricane went in a different direction. The next day, Abby told Robert she stayed upstairs the whole time, giving his ex-wife and her sister the downstairs space. Abby said she heard them whispering about the bedroom Abby was in, and how they were plotting to take over the room and put Abby downstairs. Hearing this made Robert very angry. After Abby had opened her heart for them, thinking only about their safety, how could they think that way? He knew that if his kids weren't involved, he would have followed his instincts and not agreed to have his ex-wife stay over.

Robert felt Jessica and her sister's behavior was unnecessary and unacceptable—particularly their destructive minds and immature actions, ridiculing Abby for her kindness. It stunned Robert that Jessica would react to Abby's kindness in the manner she did, after saying she had been saved and carrying on like a saint in church.

She was like a rainbow of different colors; and she let her sister fill her mind with ideas that left a disagreeable taste in his mouth. He thought he knew this woman; instead, he had to reconsider his way of thinking of her irresponsible behavior that trapped Abby in a house of horror. Abby's kindness was not only on the surface; it was in her heart, and it showed in her concern for his kids.

Jessica's erratic behavior made Robert feel even closer to Abby, and he embraced his relationship with her with the utmost respect a man could have for a woman. And he liked everything about her—her looks, her figure, and the way she walked, which really turned him on.

They had a romantic relationship that left a thirst for each other, and never did he get tired of making love to her. They later moved from New Orleans East to another section of town called the Carrollton on S. Claiborne Avenue, where Abby discovered she was pregnant.

As with any woman, the word *marriage* was in the back of her mind, and it was a word that wasn't in Robert's vocabulary. He was still going through the aftermath of the roller-coaster ride of his previous marriage, and these days, marriage to him was like trying to go upstream in a boat without a paddle.

Under the circumstances, he regarded marriage as a great challenge that left no room for a commitment, and with his unstable mind, more and more each day, it turned into a subject that held him hostage because of Abby's pregnancy. He went through the motions of agreeing to the marriage when his heart was so far away.

He wanted the baby because of his love for Abby, but his perception of marriage, because of her pregnancy, was overwhelming and reminded him of his previous marriage for the same reason. He wanted her to be happy, but giving her a marriage would only be giving in to her fantasy. For Robert's experience had left a scar in his subconscious mind that made him a very cautious man, not even knowing how his own fear was buried so deep. Marriage to him was a prescription label, with no refills.

He didn't want to jeopardize his relationship by hiding his fear of getting married again. Abby was so energetic and excited about her pregnancy. But he couldn't help but wonder if her pregnancy was her way of getting a commitment from him—a commitment that would keep them together forever, a commitment that would leave no interference or allow any threat of him leaving her for another woman.

In his mind, she appeared as though she had hit the lottery. She had the winning ticket, and it was time to cash it in. He knew she was only dreaming, and each day he would only think of how he could get out of this predicament, hoping time would make her have a change of heart about marriage. Obviously, having never been married before, it was a big excitement for her; for him, getting married again would only be a mirror of his past.

Robert chuckled to himself, thinking that instead of getting married again, he would have been better off going fishing. If he caught the wrong fish, it was so easy to throw it back into the water. Instead, he felt he was on a hook that was too hard to bite and too big to swallow. It was devastating for him to even think of the word *marriage*. And her way of thinking wasn't in agreement with his.

His mind filled with so many thoughts. He plotted and looked for the right combination, the right words in his defense and to steer her mind in a different direction.

Abby finally gave birth to a baby girl, whom she named Tasha. Yes, Tasha was a sight for sore eyes. God couldn't have given them a more beautiful child; she was absolutely gorgeous.

Abby was surrounded with so much attention it didn't take long before she thought she was in control and would have things her way. Carol, the next-door neighbor, had a boyfriend named Larry who thought Tasha was very cute. Carol wanted to be her godmother, and Larry asked to be her godfather. Tasha was really an adorable baby; in fact, she was an angel with a smile you could never forget.

After Tasha's birth, marriage had become even more of a significant topic and further electrified Abby's desire to be married. The more she mentioned marriage, the more irritated he felt, as though a bad rash had started to spread all over his body, with no relief in sight. Her overstuffed mind was filled with thoughts of a new life, a new beginning, a changed mind, and a different name. A name he wasn't ready to give and a life that he was undoubtedly uncertain of.

Abby was getting very excited about getting married, broadcasting the news to all members of her family, even to the point of having her stepmother to mail her birth certificate for their marriage license. Robert still couldn't see himself getting married again. He was still having flashbacks of his first marriage.

Many weeks had passed, and Abby was waiting impatiently for her birth certificate to get married. All Robert could think of was finding a way to disengage her thoughts from marriage, thoughts that were wedged so deep in her mind. His love for her and the baby was unconditional, but the word *marriage* was overpowering. For someone who had just gotten out of a divorce, this was like getting out of one grave and into another. He wasn't ready to be buried again in another situation he wasn't sure of. Still, trying to find the words to tell her he didn't want to get married was like finding a needle in a haystack.

In his subconscious mind, he was branded for life after going through a marriage that was filled with cheating and lies. He was certain that going through another marriage he was uncertain of would only be a repeat of his previous marriage. A marriage that was unthinkable, a marriage that was hard for him to inhale, and a marriage that left him breathless.

Upon the arrival of Abby's birth certificate, she was very excited, knowing that being married was now only a step away. But as for Robert, he was being pushed out of an airplane without a parachute. He was not prepared to make the jump. In his mind, he knew the proper thing to do was tell her he wasn't ready to make another commitment.

Instead, he snapped. One day, while he was babysitting Tasha, he decided to give Abby's birth certificate to the baby, helping her to tear it up into small pieces. Or more precisely, tearing it up and putting the blame on Tasha.

His idea was to tell Abby the baby got her birth certificate and tore it up in pieces. His cowardly way of putting the whole thing on Tasha was compounded with guilt, but in his mind, putting the blame on Tasha was fine, because Tasha didn't have to sleep with Abby in bed. But that was his story, and he was sticking to it. Besides, Tasha was too young to talk and too young to testify against her daddy. Yes, to him, she was really a daddy's baby.

Now, trying to convince Abby was a different story. Rehearsing his story before Abby got home from work was really getting more devastating and harder each time. His story was a long way from being perfect for her to believe. As he sat in the living room with Tasha, waiting patiently and listening for her car in the driveway, he tried to be on his best behavior, hiding his nervousness.

Eventually, he heard her car slowly pulling into the driveway. Meanwhile, trying to put his thoughts together was getting more confusing, because his story was filled with guilt. He thought boldly that she couldn't prove otherwise.

When she entered through the front door, he felt a tingle go down his throat, and his mind went totally blank when he went to greet her. Meanwhile, Tasha was overjoyed, almost jumping out of his arms, happy to see her mother, as though she had something to tell her. Robert was glad Tasha couldn't talk, and he hoped his guilt wouldn't manifest itself.

He knew he had to tell her in a timely manner about Tasha tearing up her birth certificate, hoping she would believe his story. He decided to tell her after dinner; a full stomach wouldn't give her too much room to exhaust her frustration. And because Abby was a marijuana user, he could get her to relax after dinner before he would tell her.

He waited patiently after dinner, watching her getting high, until her eyes started to get red and grow smaller and start to close. Sedated under the influence of marijuana, she kept smiling. He braced himself to tell her how Tasha had crawled into the living room and pulled out a bunch of papers from under the end table and torn them up. He told her of how Tasha had torn up her birth certificate. The smile on Abby's face faded when she heard about her birth certificate.

It was a mystery to her how Tasha could get under the end table and target only her birth certificate among other papers.

Being prepared for the swift moment, he chuckled, nodded his head, and said, "She didn't tear up only your birth certificate. She tore up some of my important papers as well." He left no room for the conflicting story that she was searching for. He was playing Tasha's attorney, defending her by saying she was only a baby and didn't know any better and didn't know what she was doing. Defending Tasha was the least he could do.

After Abby had waited for her birth certificate for so long, waiting for another one was out of the question, leaving her only room to fantasize. Somehow she felt at that point that he had no interest in marriage because of his reaction to Tasha tearing up her birth certificate. Being uncertain about their relationship, he started to investigate her every move, even her phone conversations. His past had started to surface.

Being a deputy sheriff, he decided to tap his home phone so he could keep track of whom she talked to when he wasn't home at night. The first night after the tap had been put in, she had very little conversation on the phone. The second night, he heard her conversation with the guy who supplied her with marijuana.

She called him in reference to buying more marijuana, and he asked her if she was coming over to give him some, meaning sex, as though they had had the same conversation before. He told her he was hot for her and how bad he wanted her.

Abby replied in a soft voice, as though she was enjoying every minute of his lust. "You are not hot for me. I was just calling to see if you had anything."

Robert couldn't comprehend how she would let him disrespect her with such a conversation. He waited until the next day before he approached her regarding the conversation she had with Tom, her supplier.

What made things even worse was that when he approached her, she denied having any conversation like the one he told her she had with Tom. He was just a fraction away from leaving her, but his daughter was the biggest influence on him to stay. Having solid evidence closed all doors and left no room for doubts. He always followed his training as a deputy sheriff.

He decided to let her listen to her recorded conversation with Tom, leaving her breathless and leaving no room for discussion. Abby felt as though she had been stripped naked, her true character exposed. Acting purely out of reflex, she roughly grabbed and snapped the tape, destroying it little by little, piece by piece, this evidence that filled the room with guilt. Robert knew she knew marriage was now out of the question.

His suspicion of her of having skeletons in her closet proved he was right to be wary of a commitment he would regret, a commitment that would put him back in the shadows of his past. After she had destroyed the tape, she edited it in her own words, as though she was giving herself a way out and a softer pillow to sit on.

After listening to the tape over and over, Robert felt he didn't have to listen to it again, because every word had been etched in his mind, and there was nothing she could say to ease the pain. She wasn't upset about her conversation with Tom; she was upset by his technique of being the fly on the wall behind closed doors, listening to her phone conversation, which she thought was in private.

Her conversation with Tom was a subject she couldn't put to rest. Every time her relatives came around, her conversation about Tom would always come up, as though Robert didn't hear what he had heard and it was only a delusion. She always had to try to explain herself to someone, hiding what had happened, putting herself on trial.

It was like cancer eating away at her each time it crossed her mind. Her attitude toward him was a sign of guilt, and it was hard for her to accept that she had been caught with her hand in the cookie jar, even though she was trying to sweep away the crumbs that would leave a trail, to help her stay in complete denial.

She acted as though it was a nightmare, a billboard that was painted with many ugly colors that was reaching out to destroy her, her narrow mind putting her on stage in a spotlight filled with frustration from stepping on the shattered glass surrounding her. Robert would minister to his own mind. He would never worry about things he had no control of, and he would forget things that of no value and move on with his life, because the elements of being unhappy had many rooms in which to fantasize about things that would only destroy him. Nevertheless, in his mind, he knew what a man could gain, as well as what he could lose; and what he lost, he could always recover.

He was absolutely sure *marriage* was only a word of the past, but he had to expand his mind and go on as though nothing had happened. His love for her and the baby still filled the air with a fragrance that was precise and unconditional, that overpowered her faults.

On June 25, 1984, he received a Certificate of Merit from the mayor of New Orleans. It read,

> Be it known that for outstanding service, the mayor
> of New Orleans has conferred this certificate of merit
> upon Deputy Sheriff Robert Smith.

With Robert being in the spotlight of the department, even his superior attitude started to change, as though he wanted his position right after the sheriff had announced that Robert was qualified to fill the highest-ranking position in the department.

Abby, doing her own thing—that is, smoking marijuana—always had him on pins and needles regarding someone finding out about her drug addiction.

A few years later, he found himself resigning from the sheriff's department. He no longer felt comfortable within the department. As time went on, her drug addiction spread to other things that left her uncontrollable with drugs that would destroy their relationship. Still he loved her and stood by her because of his obligation to Tasha. Not knowing he had gone beyond his expectation of digging an even deeper grave that led to another pregnancy.

Her attitude showed no anticipation of having any responsibilities toward him or Tasha, leaving him to play the role of father and mother.

Abby's irresponsible ways and her transgressions made it clear she had no real determination to overpower her addiction. On July 30, 1992, their second child was born. Abby named her Nora. Nora had more of Robert's features than any of his kids, and she was very hairy like her father.

Still, Abby had no discipline and could not overcome her drug addiction, leaving her with the same erratic behavior that distanced her from him and the kids. The truth was that her cruel and unusual punishment of Robert and the kids made Robert think that soon she was going to abandon them.

Approximately months later, after Nora was born, Robert was on the borderline, disengaging his relationship with Abby and leaving New Orleans to unscramble his mind, knowing this relationship was headed down a dead-end road that was filled with destruction. He was self-employed as a mechanic, trying to make ends meet as much as he could; but found it hard to do when majority of the time, Abby was nowhere to be found, leaving him to take care of the kids.

And it seemed as though everyone in New Orleans had turned their back on him, even his two daughters from his previous marriage. They never did care for Abby at all, but his son always reached out, showing a sign of compassion. None of his relatives, except for his son, really liked Abby and they always distanced themselves in a bizarre and sarcastic manner. And spared him no mercy for the predicament he was in.

It seemed as though every door that was open at one time had now closed, and everyone around him had hardened their heart. In his heart, Robert knew he had taken a big fall, but no hand reached out to pick him up. Not even one encouraging word to give him hope. He called his sister Julie, who lived in California, with a trembling voice and tears running down his face, and knew he had reached his limit of a predicament that left him with no money and all his material possessions now gone.

Julie, who genuinely loved her brother, reacted with no hesitation when she knew he had no money. She wired him his bus fare and money for him to buy food. He knew Julie was giving him a way out for a new beginning, but leaving his family behind was hard to do.

The money Julie had sent him for food was enough to buy Abby and his two daughter tickets to Jackson, Mississippi, where Abby's mother and father lived. That left him only bus fare to travel but none for food. He had only thirty cents in his pocket.

As Robert sat on the bus, his thoughts penetrated his heart. As he looked out of the window, staring into the darkness, with his reflection in the glass, tears started running down his cheeks, around the corners of his mouth. He could taste his own tears between his lips. In many cases the grass may appear to be greener on the other side, when the stems of the roots deep down have a coloration of being yellow.

As clear as day, God spoke to him: "I am with you, and I promise I will be with you every step of the way. Now you know what it is like to have, and now you know what it is like to have not."

After riding the bus for hours with nothing to eat, Robert started to get hungry. The bus stopped by a depot stop to pick up other passengers and give other passengers a chance to grab a snack from the vending machines. Robert remembered he had only thirty cents in his pocket, so he stepped off the bus, hoping he had enough for a bag of potato chips.

Unfortunately, everything in the machine was forty cents; he was a dime short. He was so hungry it crossed his mind to ask another passenger for a dime for the potato chips, but he had too much pride to ask anyone for anything. To his right, there was a bubble gum machine; the gum was only twenty-five cents. At this point, he just wanted anything to put in his mouth.

As he made an attempt to put the quarter in the bubble gum machine's coin slot, he realized there was some object that was just sitting in there. He reached in and caught the tip of it with his fingernail, flipping it free. It hit the floor. He glanced down and saw it was a silver dime—just what he needed to buy the potato chips. Again God spoke: "I told you, I am with you."

What God said brought chills to Robert's body because God was manifesting his word and leaving a confirmation with no doubt. He was convinced that the Lord was a miracle worker, and he felt a warmth in the palm of his hand, when God had his hand in his own, guiding him.

As Robert continued on his journey, a strange thing happened: A man came out of nowhere and asked him where he was going. Robert told him his destination was California, and that he was going there to try to start his life over.

With no hesitation, the stranger corrected him: "Don't say try. Say you're going to California to start your life all over." It was as though he knew all about Robert and what he had been through. Then the man said, "I have some bread and a cooler with some meat in it. When you get hungry, you can fix yourself a sandwich."

Again, the tears from Robert's heart welled out of his eyes, because once again, God had shown him his present.

After a few hours, the stranger got off the bus. He shook Robert's hand, looked at him with warmth, and said, "You're not going to California to try to start your life over, but you *will* start over a new life."

Robert now had only a short distance to travel. And God had made his present visible, leaving no room for doubt. To him, the whole thing was so strange; he wondered if he had just met an angel in the image of a man.

God was truly in control. Without a doubt, he was the pilot, and Robert was just there for the ride. He thought of something he had read: "It's not how far or fast of a distance you may travel, but the distance you travel from where you started from." He knew he had to achieve his goals. His feelings for Abby were only an imprint of the past, and his anticipation of being with her again left him with no desire to celebrate.

In California, it didn't take him long to blend in. He found a job working with inmates in a work release facility. In addition, he sought employment with the Orange County Sheriff's Department. The cost of living in Los Angeles was entirely too high, not allowing him to save anything. He was uncertain as to whether he wanted to establish a future there.

Being human, he couldn't help but wonder about his family. He still had feelings for Abby. He braced himself for a life that had no part in the situation that God had brought him out of. He got in touch with an old girlfriend. Marie was a married woman, but he still considered her a good friend. He enjoyed his conversations with her, which took his mind off Abby.

His everyday conversations with her encountered an obsession that brought both of them to a romantic atmosphere. He just wanted someone to love; his warm generosity to her left him no room to discriminate on her marital status.

He remembered an old saying: "To forget an old love, find a new one." Abby wasn't even a prominent subject in his thoughts anymore; thoughts of her now felt like a bad rash. Marie gave him the impression her marriage was on the rocks, and that being disloyal to her husband wasn't just a flaw but a way of betraying him. It was as though she was trying to get even.

She would always tell Robert how much she loved him, but he felt that even though the mouth spoke it, the heart was so far away. Robert felt he was just an inspiration for her to be able to get up the nerve to escape her marriage, but material things were standing in her way. At the time, Marie and her husband were getting a new home built. She tried to convince Robert the house didn't mean anything to her. Slowly but surely, his feelings for her started to grow, and every minute of their phone conversation assured him she was serious about their relationship.

A short time after starting a relationship with Marie, Robert noticed how she and Abby had a lot in common, singing the same old familiar song *marriage*, which convinced him she did love him. In his mind, he felt he would really marry her too. She put the icing on the cake by buying him a wedding band, even though she was still confined in her marriage.

The sensation of being in love and loving again was a wonderful feeling, which motivated him even more so to be with her. But California was a distasteful environment filled with many mishaps that left him incapable to fulfill the goal he wanted to achieve.

Robert talked to his sister Sally, who lived in Doraville, Georgia. She asked him to come live and work in Georgia, which would bring him closer to Marie, who lived only about eight hours away. When Marie heard he was moving to Georgia, she was overcome with joy and made arrangements to meet him there.

After only a few days upon his arrival in Georgia, Marie met him at a hotel. She greeted him with a red rose, which really put him in a romantic atmosphere. She was so sexy and attractive, and looking at her as though he had x-ray vision, his thoughts had already put her in bed, and no bedtime story was needed.

He couldn't seem to stop kissing her, and she dazzled him with her charm and showered him more love than any man could ask for. She knew she was holding his heart hostage, and the ransom was to love her for eternity. She was like a vampire, draining his body with love, leaving him breathless, and with just enough strength to nod. He enjoyed the precious time they shared together and her remarkable attitude, which made him want to pamper her forever. And if this was a dream, he didn't want to wake up.

But their present together was about to come to an end after spending the weekend. And saying good-bye was very hard to do. A swift current of sadness moved in his heart, like the wind electrifying his whole body. He did not know when he would see her again. He had gotten so addicted to her—just being in her presence, lost in her touch, her kiss that filled his heart with a feeling he hadn't felt in a long time. He found himself listening to any music that would remind him of her, and he thought of her every minute of the day.

A short time later, a company called the Asset Protection Team, out of Virginia, sought security officers to travel from state to state. Knowing Marie was thinking of divorcing her husband prompted him with more initiative and self-discipline to find a job to establish a better relationship for him and her. The incentive of their relationship filled his mind with a picture painted in bright colors that would never fade.

After a few days had passed, he was informed he was hired by Asset Protection Team and was given a date to start training for his position.

His relationship with Marie grew more and more each day, leaving him with a positivity imprint that would never diminish. His love for her left him witless, blocking out the fact that she was still a married woman, and that she was letting his immature heart control his naked eye. He started training for his new job in Atlanta, Georgia, which lasted approximately one week.

Upon completion of his training, his first job assignment was at Kaiser Aluminum in Louisiana. He had worked in Louisiana only for a few days when his assignment there was canceled. Instead of letting the company fly him back to Atlanta, he flew into Jackson, Mississippi, to meet Marie.

She picked him up from the airport with loving arms and pampered him in a way that filled him with a thirst for her love and affection. Their attraction for each other was stronger than ever, which led them to the closest hotel, where they filled their room with passion.

Still, he couldn't help but wonder if she would change her mind upon the completion of the new home she and her husband were having built. But he knew he had to block his negative thoughts to achieve his goals and allow their relationship to grow. And planting a bad seed would produce only a bad relationship. Robert stayed in Jackson for only a very short time since he was asked to go on another job assignment in Peoria, Illinois.

Upon his arrival in Peoria, Robert started to experience a weird sickness. He had dizzy spells that caused him to walk close to the walls just to keep his balance. The ground he walked on was spinning like a merry-go-round, and he had to grab the stair rails as he walked up and down the stairs. Each day he clawed and struggled for survival, hiding his sickness from his employer and Marie.

His blood pressure was normal. Being out of work for a few weeks, he was determined not to fly back home with his sickness after working for thirty days and living in misery from his dizzy spells. Then suddenly, his dizziness just disappeared.

His anticipation over flying into Peoria encouraged him to build a solid foundation of his finances that would lead to the material things he wanted them to have. A short time later, talking to Marie over the phone, he felt the tension in her voice and noticed her unpleasant attitude when she informed him that the home she and her husband were having built had been completed. Right then, from the sound of her voice, he knew the material things in her marriage undoubtedly was rooted more in her mind than the love in her heart for him.

He knew he loved her and never wanted to accept that he had to live in the shadows of the memory of the love they once had.

Robert himself wondered whether he himself was using her to help him get over Abby. And now who would help him get over Marie? He felt as though he was in a merry-go-round. Spinning too slow to achieve what he wanted and spinning too fast with passion for him to jump off.

His thoughts were paralyzed; he didn't know which way to go, and he did not even have one friend to talk to. He had less time for sympathy and less time to sit around feeling sorry for himself. He knew his heart was holding him hostage in a relationship he had no control of. Deep down in his heart, he knew it was time to turn the page.

He wondered, how could a man withstand so many disappointments and expect to live with high expectations when so many things stood in his way? He knew he had the right combination of being consistent and having ambition, which was what he needed to overpower anything he might encounter. His situation brought him back to what God had told him—that he was with him, and knowing where God had brought him from left no room for doubts.

Even at Robert's weakest moments, God still kept his promise and highly favored him. Robert prayed, "Lord, please teach me how to pray and stand fast through my good and my bad." His thoughts brought him back to Adam and Eve: once again, a woman had brought him into the garden of forbidden fruit, in a zone that he had trespassed, cheating with a married woman. He knew he had to brace himself with positive thoughts, with smiles that would cover the frown that was buried so deep within him. Throughout all this, he never wavered in his conviction that God still highly favored him.

And even in the moments of his silent storms, the sun shone right on through. He resolved to stay on course, to overpower his personal emotions in order to explore the better things in life for him and his kids. With no doubt, life would still go on, whether one is on this earth or buried beneath it. For every leaf that falls from a tree, a new leaf will bud; and for every flower that dies, a new flower will bloom, and through all our trials and our tribulations, life still goes on.

CHAPTER 5

Mary, The Second Wife

ROBERT FOLLOWED HIS INSTINCTS, TAKING each day at a time, releasing the tension, working long hours to block his past of being out at sea, riding the tall waves of rough and stormy relationships that showed no mercy. Many people knew his name, but none knew of the shadows of his past. He kept a close relationship with his kids, which brought him back in contact with their mothers. First, Abby, and then for some reason, his ex-wife wanted to revive a relationship she had left behind years ago.

In his mind, he knew where God had brought him from, which reminded him of 2 Peter 2:22. "But it is happened unto them according to the true proverb. The dog turned to his own vomit again; and the sow that was washed to her wallowing in the mire."

There are many things that God would let us go through, though we don't know the reason why. Robert's relationship with Marie helped him to have a neutral relationship with Abby, putting him to the test and confirming that now he could go on without her, walking out of the shadows of his past.

He thought of his ex-wife and how there were too many years between them, and he remembered an old saying: "Time will heal all wounds." He no longer thought of or felt anything for either Abby or Jessica. The only thing they had in common was that they were mothers of his kids. Abby called him to tell him she went to a rehabilitation center just for him, because she wanted him back.

With no hesitation, he told her, "Don't go to rehab for me. Go for yourself. If you don't go for yourself, it will never work. You have to want something to mollify your lifestyle—not for me but for yourself. Don't beguile yourself with false promises that will distract you from your goals and have you setting yourself up for failure."

And on the other side of the world, his ex-wife had just gone to school to become a registered nurse, throwing material things at him, selling herself with high praise, trying to bait him. Robert scratched his head, but there were no conflicting emotions that highlighted his thoughts. He realized that a man who set his sense of greed beyond his limitation was a man who was setting himself up to self-destruct. All his life, he always had too much pride to take anything from any woman.

One thing she said would be imprinted in his mind for the rest of his life. She said the worst thing she could have ever done in her life was leaving him, even though she confessed to leaving him for another man for no reason, because she had no knowledge of Robert's relationship with Teresa. Besides, he would have never left her for another woman. And even when he wanted to forgive her, she closed her ears, hardened her heart, and shielded her emotions with an untouchable attitude.

Still, Robert kept in mind his religious beliefs. In God's eyes, his first wife would always be his wife until death did them part. He wrestled with himself because of his beliefs, and he thought of the material things he could gain. He tried to convince himself to go back to his wife. His aunt had told him what he already knew: that on judgment day, he would have to answer to God as to why he didn't stay with his wife.

He wrestled and wrestled with himself. He knew he didn't love her anymore. And going back for the sake of material things wouldn't be fair to her, and to himself. And knowing he had cheated, when he did love her at one time, and not loving her would only put him through a revolving door, a repetition of cheating, over and over, because there was no love involved.

After Abby had gone through rehab for thirty days, a week or two later, she was back to her old habits, engaging her drug addiction, showing no regard for herself or for the kids. Just the thought of his kids kept Robert on edge. Not knowing what might happen to them kept him restless. The kids' grandmother called him, saying, "Robert, you need to come and get the kids."

Abby was walking the streets with her baby girl, Nora, all times of the night, trying to support her drug habit. He didn't understand how Abby's mother could let her take the kids when he had legally taken the kids out of Abby's custody, giving the grandmother full custody. And what really pierced his heart was that the baby girl, at the age of three, was saying, "Daddy, please come and get me."

And he prayed to God to keep them and teach him how to go and get them, knowing he was traveling from state to state on jobs assignment, sometimes for as long as five months. He knew he had to find a way to go and get them, because if something happened to them, his baby girl's voice would haunt him for the rest of his life: *Daddy, please come and get me.* Robert knew he had to do something fast. A thought came to mind: if he had to marry a bear to help him pull his kids out of the jaws of danger, then so be it. He had to get them out of harm's way.

On assignment in Peoria at Caterpillar, Robert met a girl named Mary. She had five kids, with one child still at home. She worked at Caterpillar cleaning up the buildings there. His job had strict rules prohibiting him from fraternizing with the opposite sex, releasing the company he worked for from the liability of a sexual harassment suit.

He liked her because of her appearance, and she had such an innocent and a sweet, calm attitude about her. He told her of his job's strict rules and not being able to communicate with her in public. She gave him her phone number, knowing that was the only way he could communicate with her.

He learned she had some strong religious beliefs, which made him pursue her even more. She was married but had been separated from her husband for a while. They talked every night, and their conversations brought them even closer. She presented herself as an angel, and she'd had a bad experience with her husband cheating on her with another woman.

Never once did she take the blame for anything, putting herself onstage with no faults. Still, there was something about her; he just couldn't put his heart into it. Her devastating story about how her husband treated her was consistent; it was as though she was looking for his sympathy to win him over. It appeared to him she was covering up her own fault by painting an image of herself as a save and sanctified woman of God. She painted a bright and loud-colored picture of her husband as a deceiving and conniving man, with scandal and disgrace to his name. She told him about how he was cheating on her, and how she ended up keeping the other woman's kids after the woman's house caught on fire. She painted herself as meek and humble. She had to be the angel that was missing in heaven.

Her smile was eye-catching, and her personality drew people to her like a magnet; they believed whatever she said. But what puzzled Robert the most was how a woman with such a personality and being as attractive as she was had no man in her life. Peoria was a small town, where everyone knew everybody; and if she was a good catch, why wasn't she in someone else's arms? Instead, she was too busy criticizing her husband. It was really a mystery to him. Telling her a little about his past and his kids opened her heart with passion and concerns.

A short time later, his assignment in Peoria came to an end, and upon his departure, he made arrangements for her to pick him up at the airport so he could spend time with her before flying out of Peoria.

She picked him up and showed him more of the town, and eventually, she took him to her house. Walking into her house, he saw how even the place where she lived had no faults, clean as a pin.

Robert loved the way Mary carried herself and the cleanness of her house. He couldn't help thinking how different she was from his first wife, from the way Jessica had kept their home—dust so heavy he could write his name on the drawer and how when he reached under the bed for his shoes he pulled out a chicken bone instead. Mary was so organized and knew how to keep a house. He braced himself and resolved not to make any sexual advances toward her.

He liked everything about her, but she didn't give him that impression of being sexy—she was very neat and clean, but not sexy. She didn't give him that spark that made him want to get in bed with her, but he had to test the waters. He tried to kiss her, and she turned her cheek with a slight smile. And again, time wasn't on his side. He had to get back to the airport to catch his flight.

He flew to Atlanta, Georgia, and they still kept close contact. She appeared to be everything a man could want a woman to be, but he couldn't feel any strong feelings for her. He liked her a lot, and his communication with her was consistent with having someone to talk to. Besides, he had no one else in his life, and she kept him from being bored.

What was even more devastating was when she said she would help him take care of his kids. He knew he had to go to get his kids sooner or later, and he was aware of his predicament with his kids and how his job wouldn't allow him to be at home with them.

But like everything else, her offer came with a price tag, and she gave him the impression she too was seeking marriage and was using his kids as a master key to a commitment.

It didn't take long for Robert to read through to the fine print. Because of her religious beliefs, shacking up was out of the question. He knew she wanted marriage from the things she would say, about how she would take care of her husband, and he would never have to worry about her cheating on him.

It seemed as though she knew she had him against the rope, knowing he couldn't take care of his kids alone, and so his kids were being used as bargaining tools. And she gave him the impression she was horny and wanted a man in her bed with no shame—a sex buffet, where she could have as much as she wanted and didn't have to worry about her church, and didn't have to repent and worry about God's approval, where she was cleared from committing fornication.

She had blocked out the fact of adultery, which meant she was still a married woman as well. Marriage gave her all the fringe benefits of having a man in her bed to ease her conscience, of being free from sin and still being able to engage in sexual activities beneath the covers, and staying in good standing in the eyes of her church. In the shadows of his religious beliefs, her first husband would always be her husband; and his first wife would always be his wife.

He stirred her pot by telling her how much he loved her, but his heart was so far away. His tongue spoke of love, but the right ingredients were missing. But having the right ingredients wasn't on her agenda. Deep down, he knew she knew he didn't love her, but it didn't matter. She just wanted a husband, and he needed a mother to take care of his kids.

Then again, he remembered what he had decided: to give his kids the right support, he would marry a bear. But then he kept in mind that marrying Mary was a long way from marrying a bear. He could grow to love her. But he was getting cold feet again; the idea of getting married again was hard to digest. In Robert's subconscious mind, he was really frightened to get married again.

Talking to Mary on the phone, he actually fell in love with her, but the feeling was not enough to penetrate his heart to make him long for marriage. But to give their relationship a chance, he left Atlanta and went to Chicago, to go live with his mother which put him close to Mary. His mother remarried to a guy named Richard and his mother given birth another girl named Keisha. Robert's step father died years later before Keisha finish high school.

After being in Chicago a few days, Mary drove from Peoria to spend some time with him. He found himself liking her even more—more now than the first time they were together in Peoria. What was so remarkable was that his mother got a chance to meet her as well. He knew his mother would put up very little objection, or none at all, because of Mary's easygoing attitude. Mary quickly grabbed his mother's attention, who called her a sweet person. The day they shared together was filled with happiness.

At the conclusion of their day, when they were finally behind closed doors, the room filled with their darkest thirst, their heated passion, taking her out of practice of her religious belief. Robert hoped to feel enough sexual desire for her that would elevate his feelings for her.

In the midst of making love to her, she went into a motion of different expressions of knowing she had fallen outside of the guidelines of her religion. The aftermath of their sexual activity swiftly filled the room with guilt, but it still left her horny, wanting sex more and more, with less of a conscience. In Robert's mind, he could hear her say, "Oh my God."

The expression on her face indicated she was sinning and repenting at the same time.

Frankly, to him, their sexual activity left him with less desire for her; he was more turned off than on. He thought about the pureness of her heart, and of searching for someone else who might be better in bed but with less of a heart.

And he was looking at her heart and the rest, hoping to grow in a relationship that had to be tailor-made to fit, willing to close his eyes to all her faults and to accept the things he couldn't change.

All the days of his life, Robert had never seen a woman with such a heart that exercised so much concern for him and others. Putting more icing on the cake, she would mention his kids repeatedly, reminding him she would help him take care of them.

For some reason, he felt she knew he was at one of his weakest moments with his kids, and she knew the right combination that would make him give in to the temptation of marrying her. He felt deep within that she knew he didn't love her, but she didn't care. Again Robert's job called him to another assignment in Illinois. During the whole time he was gone, he received letters from her quite often. For the first time, he noticed that her education had been very poor, as evidenced by her letters. It made him deliberate more as to being her protector and mentor, being there to help her with things she was incapable of, encouraging him to accept her for better or worse.

His thoughts were interrupted by a flashback that made him hear his daughter's voice saying "Daddy, come and get me." He was still having heavy, cloudy thoughts about getting married again. And he didn't want his love for his kids to make him do something that would fill him with regret the rest of his life.

After hearing less and less from Abby's mother asking him to come get his kids, he assumed that maybe Abby had straightened up her act, freeing his mind from thoughts of marriage.

He visualized just taking his time and tiptoeing through a relationship he wasn't sure of. Mary was still a mystery—a woman who was so nice and yet had a one-track mind and wanting marriage so badly.

His conversations with her over the phone enticed him with her unique attitude of being so meek and humble, convincing him that she was a good woman. On one occasion, she mentioned that her phone bill was due and that she didn't have the money to pay it. Without hesitation, and out of the kindness of his heart, Robert offered to pay it. He mailed her the full amount to avoid any interruption in her phone service. She ensured him she would use the money to pay her phone bill.

After a couple of weeks had passed, her conversation led her speaking with a fast, loose tongue, stating she had to pay her phone bill. Robert lashed out at her: "I sent you the money to pay your phone bill, and you assured me you did." That caught her in a lie, and she fell silent. Right at that moment, Robert felt a lack of trust in her.

Immediately, she got very apologetic for lying to him. Right at that moment, Robert felt that his religious girl had started to grow the horns of Satan, showing her true colors, being a rattlesnake, ready to strike. Mary was drowning herself with regrets, trying to retrieve the trust he had in her and hoping he would overlook what she did and forgive her. He couldn't help thinking of his past, but he refused to let the past be his future. He wanted to consider the past as a learning experience.

Robert braced himself and reorganized his thoughts, coming up with a different scenario where he could forgive her, hoping to achieve a relationship where trust could be rehabilitated without conflicting emotions in dealing with the darkness of his conscience. He gave her the benefit of the doubt, not looking back at yesterday and having positive thoughts for today.

After being gone for sixty days, Robert returned to Chicago. What he felt for Mary in his heart was still a numb feeling, unanswered. Like flower lacking sun and water, it just wouldn't blossom.

He didn't love her, but he loved the way she carried herself—very clean and neat and more of a mother figure to his kids. She drove to Chicago every chance she got to spend time with him. In an indirect way, she would have this gleaming smile, raising her eyebrow and demonstrating possession of him, reminding him of his kids and how she would help him take care of them. She was banking on his kids legally binding them in a commitment of marriage.

Still, Robert couldn't even visualize being prepared for marriage again after being in two other relationships and a marriage that left a stain of regrets. He had to discipline himself to avoid hurting Mary's feelings and to escape her pursuit of marriage. He struggled with the wrong reason of marrying her just for his kids' sake, which would have him playing the role of a husband, when the truth was she was just his babysitter. She really didn't care, as long as he was in her bed with her every night, playing the role of her husband.

After another short stay in Chicago, Robert was called on another assignment in Arizona to provide security for the Smithsonian out of

Washington, DC, while the Smithsonian was on tour. He had been there in Arizona about forty-five days when his daughter's grandmother called again and told him he needed to come and get the kids because of Abby's drug addiction.

He geared himself up to go get his kids. Abby's oldest daughter, Amanda, whom she had before she met Robert, told him she wasn't going to let him take the kids. And the kids didn't carry his last name, and his name wasn't on their birth certificates. And Abby was supporting her daughter's decision.

Amanda told him over the phone that he couldn't come to get them because his older daughter didn't want to come with him. Robert knew it was going to be a battle getting the kids; he had to get an attorney for reinforcement.

He argued with Amanda. "When I leave Arizona, I will be there to get my kids. Meanwhile, you do what you have to do, and I will do what I have to do, but I will be there to get my kids." He laid down his demands, leaving no doubt that he refused to be intimidated.

The least of Robert's worries was proving the kids were his and proving their mother was an unfit mother. For his kids, he was ready to go to battle. Abby knew he wasn't joking, and that he wasn't making a threat but a promise. He knew she was still having flashbacks in her mind when he took legal action from a distance, taking the kids away from her and placing them in their grandmother's custody. Amanda knew what he was capable of doing with regard to his kids.

When Mary heard about the commotion, she supported him, because they had already deliberated about his kids, and she was willing to help him. Mary was getting child support from her previous marriage, but she hadn't gotten a divorce yet. She knew she had no time for a long, drawn-out divorce, trying to get maintenance or any other marital asset that would give her a lesser chance of getting married to him; and timing was everything for her now.

She went to a paralegal service to file for divorce, asking for no maintenance and no marital asset. Robert thought the reason she didn't want anything was that she believed she had caught a bigger fish and therefore was willing to throw the smaller one back.

Her ex-husband agreed to her terms without hesitation. It was as though he was glad to be free of her. It was like having a surgical incision, releasing him from his pains. Mary's husband's actions left Robert wondering if the mismanagement of their relationship was really entirely his fault as Mary said—or was she making up the whole thing?

Mary kept him in the loop regarding her swift movement of obtaining her divorce. In a matter of weeks, her divorce was final, and she was free to do as she pleased. She acted as though she had risen from the dead and was ready to live again.

And she knew marriage was in the center of their relationship because of the situation with his kids leaving him totally defenseless. Robert's misfortune was definitely her dream. At once, she acted on her excitement and started planning for a big wedding; but little did she know that time wasn't on his side for advertising such a wedding.

Robert knew his assignment would end in a few weeks, which left him with a short time to plan for an attorney, and time now had been stretched for any modifications for plans for a big wedding, with so many things he has to put in place in preparation for getting his kids from Abby.

For the duration of his assignment, Robert returned to Chicago, to his mother's house. He explained to her what was going on, and she suggested bringing the kids to Chicago. Her suggestion sounded good, but knowing his mother was not in the best of health, he didn't want to put obligations on her. She disapproved of the idea of him getting married, knowing he was doing it only for his kids.

Robert knew that if he brought Abby to court, he had to prove without a shadow of a doubt that he was able to take care of their kids. And even with the job he had traveling, the kids would be going to a better home for their own interest. He was thinking of his kids with marriage in range, but he was still out of focus in visualizing himself being married again.

His overcrowded mind left him only room for action. Negotiating with Abby or her daughter left him with zero tolerance. Mary was overwhelmed and was in such a hurry to get married. Putting more pressure on him out of frustration, leaving him no room to deliberate on whether marriage was the only way he could take care of his kids. Mary's rapturous attitude left him visualizing her in the grip of joy, dancing to a song that needed no lyrics.

Greatly concerned, his mother asked him, "Why are you doing this when you know you're not ready for marriage?" She asked Mary to give him room to breathe, to stop putting so much pressure on him, telling her that if he said he was going to marry her, then he would do just that and she didn't have to keep pressuring him the way she did. Robert loved his kids, but he was having second thoughts about marriage. He could not see a light at the end of the tunnel. He struggled with himself, examining his feelings for Mary. His mind drifted as he looked for another alternative to avoid marrying her.

Just the thought of having his kids with him overpowered the fear of marrying her. He was willing to sacrifice his happiness for the kids' welfare. It was hard for him to even visualize being married when he and Mary had nothing in common. Even in bed, he was just playing the role and going through the motions.

He asked himself, could the darkness of his conscience have kept him from loving again, and had his ability to love been buried in the cemetery of his previous relationships? Analyzing his love for her, he realized he felt very little to none. What he felt for her had no value at all. He tried to psych himself out: if he married her, he could grow to love her.

Meanwhile, he felt he was in a power play with Abby and her daughter. He refused to let them dictate the well-being of his kids, knowing what type of environment they were in. The coldness of their heart seemed to be more important than what was best for the kids. The softest of his purified heart gave him the strength to stand for his kids, because they were in no position to stand up for themselves.

From the kids' birth, he had always kept his promise to them, because he wanted them to view him as a father who kept his word. Never once did he promise them anything that he didn't deliver. The kids knew by his words that he was coming to get them. It was just a matter of time, and they knew they could trust him.

Marrying Mary meant nothing if it meant leaving his kids before a doorway that barricaded them from hope and pushed them to the streets filled with drugs, streets with an appetite that would chew them up. As a parent, he felt it was his responsibility to overrule their mother and Amanda's decision. And he would never let them lead a life in the streets that had no pity.

Just by his actions, Mary told him, "Your kids are very blessed to have a father that loves them so." It was as though she was saying, "Marry me" and "I know you don't love me, but your unconditional love for your kids is beyond measure." She seemed to see his commitment as similar to being with her, with no doubt of him ever leaving her. And to be honest, he had never met a woman who was so supportive in all of his relationships.

He pictured in his mind how Jesus was crucified and how he sacrificed himself for the love of God's children to give them eternal life. He knew he couldn't give his kids eternal life, but he would give them a life of hope, a life that would give them a chance to better themselves for years to come, not only for themselves but their kids as well, giving them the right education that they deserved.

So many thoughts stampeded in Robert's mind regarding custody of his kids, but marriage was the main topic; and besides, bringing the kids into a different household with another woman, with whom he slept in the same bed, was devastating, and painting an image for them of his approval of an arrangement such as this.

Mary's mother was bedridden and living alone. Mary's employment at the time was taking care of her mother.

For some reason, Mary and her sisters and brothers all agreed to put their mother in a nursing home due to her condition. Robert immediately took Mary's mother's defense, disagreeing with putting her in a nursing home. "What's wrong with our home? That's your momma."

He told Mary her mother could come and live with them, and she could still continue taking care of her. He begged her not to put her mother in a home. Eventually, she agreed with him.

Finally, Robert made up his mind to marry Mary. But a big wedding wasn't in his provision; he just wanted to hurry and get it over with. His rebellious attitude about getting married was beginning to feel fake and was becoming a thing of the past. Nevertheless, he had to transform his thoughts, not for himself but for his kids. He knew his and her obsession of marriage were all for the wrong reasons.

His plan was to leave Chicago and go to Peoria, where they could get their marriage license and then have a very small wedding, with only a handful of people present. From that point on, Robert started to feel as though he had entered a zone of horror. Many spooky things began to happen. He called and made reservations at the airport to rent a car to drive to Peoria. At the car rental counter, he handed the clerk his credit card, but it was declined.

Robert was puzzled; he knew he had enough money on the card to cover the security deposit and the rental fee. He chuckled in embarrassment and gave the clerk another credit card from a different bank. But the second credit card was declined as well.

He left the airport filled with frustration. Upon his arrival back home, he called both his banks, explaining what had just happened with his credit cards. It was the same reason with both banks: Mary. The banks informed Robert they didn't know why his cards had declined. It seemed like a spiritual warfare had taken place.

He knew Mary was waiting for him in Peoria, so he called and told her what had happened. He couldn't help thinking that maybe he was being released from the trap of being married to her.

She responded at once, refusing to let credit cards stand in their way of obtaining their marriage license. She said, reaching out with an iron claw, "I am coming to get you." He had started to feel suspicious when he had started having problems with his credit cards, with two different banks being unable to explain why his credit cards had been declined.

In his mind, he started to feel this marriage wasn't meant to be. But she insisted that she would come and get him, and he finally gave in to her wishes. But he didn't want her driving on the highway alone. A day or so later, she started her journey to Chicago to pick him up. After waiting a long time for her, knowing how long it took to get from Peoria to Chicago, Robert started to get a little worried and nervous, because it never took her that long to get there.

An hour later, she arrived, stating that she was late because she had run into a barricade of road construction knocking the license plate off the front bumper of her car. Robert reflected again on his doubt about marrying her, believing even more so there was some spiritual warfare in the mix for this marriage taking place. He resolved to focus only on giving his kids a better life.

Still, his mind was full of doubts. He was ignoring the things that were happening. It was as though there was a curse. Still, with his kids on his mind, Robert insisted on going through with their plans. So they went full-speed ahead and got their marriage license, which now left them with only a date for the wedding. After getting their marriage license, they returned to Chicago to Robert's mother's house. They still had not set a date, but his mother said she could talk to her pastor to see if he could do a small ceremony after church service.

The pastor agreed to perform the ceremony, so Mary drove back to Chicago to attend the evening church service and then get married afterward. It shocked Robert when the pastor summoned them and two other witnesses to the back of the church during the service, where he told them that since they had gotten their license in Peoria, they had to get married in Peoria. This new brick wall they had run into filled Robert with many more doubts about marrying Mary.

Robert was determined to pursue his goal of getting his kids, letting nothing standing in his way, ignoring the strange things that were happening. He would focus only on his kids' well-being and not on the obstacles in his way.

Not once did it cross his mind that it could have been God's way of not giving his approval of this marriage. His deadline in getting his kids wasn't certain, but his strategy of overachieving his goal was beyond measure. He was using marriage to get his kids, and Mary was using his situation to get a husband.

Nevertheless, he knew time wasn't on his side, and it was time for phase 1 of giving his kids a home, and a stepmother who was willing to take care of them. Mary made arrangements with her pastor to have a small wedding ceremony at her church, with her sister and one of her daughters present.

Robert's present was there, but his mind was so far away. He didn't remember a single word of the ceremony, not even his vows, not even the pastor performing the ceremony. His mind was totally paralyzed; he didn't feel anything at all. He was totally in a daze.

After the wedding, Robert didn't feel like celebrating or going on a honeymoon. Instead, the very next day, he went back to Chicago to live with his mother. He was still feeling numb, playing the role but still wanting to be at a distance. Deep inside, he wanted to love his wife, but his crystal-clear heart had captured an image with only his kids in sight.

The impact of the idea of him being married to her hit him, and he found himself telling her he couldn't find their marriage license. It was as though he was telling her their marriage was invalid. He knew that wasn't the case, but he was totally in denial. He took advantage of her disorientation and started to secretly look for a way out while still being able to get his kids.

He laughed at himself, thinking, *How can a person get married and be in two separate places and two different beds and call themselves husband and wife?* From the time he left Peoria after their wedding, his bedroom was still upstairs in an attic at his mother's house, not in Peoria with her.

A few weeks had passed, and Robert was coming down to reality. He knew his place was there with her, so he decided to trust his instincts and go back to Peoria to get used to his wife before going to Mississippi to get his kids. After a month, he decided it was time to test the waters with Abby and her daughter and went to Mississippi to get his kids.

When he arrived, he firmly told Abby he was there to pick up the kids, and to his surprise, she had all the kids' clothes packed and was just waiting for him to pick them up. In fact, she went to New Orleans with him to help him to obtain the kids' birth certificates and their shot records for the schools in Peoria. Abby was very supportive.

After being in New Orleans with his other kids, Robert's ex-wife asked him why his wife was calling her house. At once, he lashed out at her. "My wife is not calling your house."

Jessica calmly quoted their home phone number, which Mary had before the marriage. She said the number appeared on her caller ID, and Robert knew she was telling the truth, because he hadn't given their home phone number out to anyone.

Immediately, he called Mary and asked her why she was calling Jessica's house. She hesitated, as though she was trying to find the right words to say. Before she could answer, he said, "You know, your number appeared on her caller ID. How would you feel about another woman calling your house? It's not right." Even at this early stage in their marriage, Mary had already started with the drama.

Her silence was a sign of guilt. Her action turned Robert off even more. Marrying her was spilled milk, and having his kids now, there was no time for regrets. He couldn't help but think this was her second step in showing her true colors. She had invaded their state of trust once again in their premature relationship, without a proper cause to do so.

At this point, Robert was really frustrated, feeling he had gotten married for nothing, preparing himself for court to seek custody of his kids. Still, deep down, he knew he still needed her because his job required him to travel a lot. Still, he felt maybe he could have gone a different route other than marriage, since getting his kids had turned out so easy. He psyched himself out and remembered marriage was their original plan before the confrontation with Abby and her daughter.

After being in Abby's presence for a little while, looking deep within her, her love for the kids penetrated his heart. He could see she loved the kids, but her drug addiction was a sickness that kept her trapped in another world. In all his days, he had never felt such sadness in his heart for her. He said, "Abby, I'm not here to take the kids from you. Just until you can get better."

The kids could always come back to their mother, but for now, taking them away was a must. She hugged the kids with tears in her eyes, hating to see them go, but she knew they were better off with their father. He promised her, leaving only his words for collateral, that he would bring them back after she had recovered from her addiction, hoping she would give rehabilitation another try and succeed this time.

He glanced at his kids and could see the sadness in their eyes, how they did not want to leave their mother behind. He looked at both of them still having so much courage despite knowing they were going to an unknown place, where they would be surrounded by unknown people, not knowing what to expect; but never once did they complain. They just followed their father's lead. Robert's heart was penetrated by their reaction, their trust in his decision.

He knew that going back to Peoria was going to be a long ride back, and he had so much on his mind—including Mary. How would she treat his kids, and how would the kids take to her and her kids? The kids' happiness was very important to him. On the way back to Peoria, he pampered them, telling them a little about Mary, making them feel a little more comfortable with her.

Before they could even make it back to Peoria, his job called him to fly out on another assignment the very next day, leaving him with only enough time to drop the kids off with Mary and then pack to catch his flight. He and the kids arrived in Peoria at 2:00 AM, and his flight was very early the same morning. He felt even worse realizing he was dropping his kids off at a total stranger's house, their father nowhere around.

Still, the kids never complained. He was so proud of them for being capable of such an understanding. He knew how hard it was for them to adjust.

CHAPTER 6

The Deaths of Robert's Father and Mother

MARY HAD BEEN WAITING FOR them. Robert could tell at her very first glance at the kids that she could tell how much the baby girl had been neglected. Robert's younger daughter was four, and the older child was twelve.

She hugged them, and then hesitated, as though she was searching for the right words to say, but she was very supportive. And even with that, Robert knew God had to take over and take the wheel, because he still didn't have any sense of direction. He prayed that God would keep them until he got back home. Mary was being very apologetic about calling Jessica's house, knowing she didn't have any reason to do so.

She really took charge of the kids, bringing them up to par, changing their image of having someone in their life who was really taking care of them.

The love he was hoping to grow in their relationship was starting to take root because of the love she had shown for his kids. Slowly but surely, he started to treasure their relationship, and he started feeling that he did the right thing in marrying her. Her actions left him with a trouble-free mind; she appeared to be more than just a wife; she was a good mother as well.

She took full control of the kids, and she took care of them better than their own mother did; and if the kids needed anything, she supplied their every need—the clothes they had on their back, even the food they ate and their school supplies. With the picture she painted, a man couldn't ask for anything more. With her easygoing ways, her being so meek and humble, she appeared to be such an angel filled with love and concern for the well-being of others.

He would call her and the kids every day, to see how they were doing. He could tell the kids were still trying to adjust; and Mary, with her pleasant attitude, seemed to be saying she had everything under control, and that she didn't want him to worry about them. She was really too good to be true. He was still in the stage of growing to love her for her positive mind, and he thought of how blessed he was to have her in his and the kids' lives.

Her kindness brought him back out of the shadows of his previous marriage and his past relationships. He couldn't help thinking, *How can you lie and not cheat, and how can you cheat and not lie?*

He told himself their marriage would leave no room for cheating and dishonesty. He was going to try to give his marriage his all. He wanted a stable relationship with a solid foundation that would stand even in the roughest times.

He was very anxious for his assignment to end so he could go home to his wife and kids, but time just stood still. He found himself bragging to his coworkers about being blessed to have a woman like Mary in his life, who was being such a mother figure to his kids. He was so happy that he had found her, and he couldn't help but feel he was in her debt for taking care of his kids.

She was truly a dream come true, and her character alone activated some feelings he was hoping would grow in their marriage. Dramatically, his fear and negative opinion about marrying her were absolutely gone. Finally, his assignment was coming to an end, and he was restless the night before, impatient to fly out the next morning to go home to his wife and his kids.

She was waiting patiently at the Peoria airport by the baggage claim. He greeted her with a kiss and a tight hug, acknowledging he was glad to see her. He was also impatient to see his kids, who weren't aware he was coming home that day. It would be a total surprise.

When they arrived home, Mary wanted some private time for herself before letting the kids know he was back. They tiptoed through the house to the bedroom, and Mary's heated passion had a thirst that couldn't wait. Her desire for him was overwhelming.

She would say, "Are you ready?" And Robert would reply, "Are you ready?" And she would say, "I stay ready." His desire for her had increased very little, and he still couldn't help but feel he had a debt to pay her for taking care of his kids. He was in such a rush to satisfy her sexual need, which left her burning with a stronger desire for him.

When he entered the kids' bedroom, it was as though so much sunshine had entered the room, and their priceless smiles penetrated his heart. Mary had both his girls looking like little dolls. He wanted to reward them for being so brave and understanding because he knew that they had been through a lot.

Then he noticed something about his older daughter being unhappy, but she remained silent. And he could sense a little jealousy in Mary when the kids would be present, but he ignored it; he just shook it off, knowing it was too premature for her to be jealous of his kids when they were around him.

Mary had five kids, and they were also amazing. They opened their hearts and welcomed his kids with open arms. In honesty, they treated his kids as though they were their real sisters, from her youngest child to the eldest. His kids couldn't have asked for more love than they were shown.

Mary's sisters had hearts of gold, lending a hand whenever they saw fit to do so. Her whole family sheltered them with so much love. For some reason, however, from day one, he felt that Mary's oldest daughter didn't like him at all; but even if it was so, her attitude with his kids never reflected any cruelty.

Robert loved Mary's kids all for the love they had shown his kids. Mary really played the role of a mother, putting the kids in school, taking all the weight off of him. His baby daughter had no knowledge at all how to count or how to recite her alphabet.

Mary, who had less schooling herself, applied all she knew to help Nora to catch up on her lessons, since Nora had been neglected because of her mother's drug addiction. Mary would help Nora with her homework each day, making that her main priority. She had so much passion for Nora, ensuring the little girl got the education she didn't get herself.

Each night she would sit at the kitchen table with Nora, working hard to improve the little girl's learning ability. Mary was really amazing, being so patient with a child who had been mismanaged and was crying out for help. All the things she had gone through with the kids, not once did she call Robert to complain—not even when she wasn't having an easy time providing for their daily needs. She appeared to have a heart as pure as gold; she was a wife who was willing to go to the limit for her husband.

The woman was too good to be true. Even when she was having problems with her family members, all she would say was, "I will pray for them." She was being very meek and humble, leaving Robert frustrated. He would say, "You can't let them do that to you." He would think, *If she doesn't go to heaven, no one will.*

Just for a few moments, Robert's mind drifted to his father during the time he was on a job assignment in Pennsylvania just before his father died. He never got a chance to meet Mary.

Robert couldn't help but remember receiving a phone call from his auntie Rose, who had been at his father's side just shortly before he died. She informed Robert his father was sick. His father had remarried a woman named Janet, who appeared to be very meek and humble but had cost his father his life. Robert's auntie Rose told him Janet had totally brainwashed his father, who loved her to a point where he had to distance himself from his family, even his kids. Robert couldn't help but remember that when he was a young boy, his father would have him sit by the water faucet to cut the water on and off as he washed his car, since his father had no nozzle to put on the end of the hosepipe. One day, the water pressure must have been low. Robert's father yelled out to him to turn the water all the way up.

Robert replied, "Daddy, it's all the way up."

Robert's father immediately told him to cut the water off, with frustration in his voice, as though Robert was the blame. He peered down the hosepipe with one eye to see if anything was jammed down the hosepipe. Right at that moment, a little voice told Robert to turn the faucet on at full blast. The little voice that Robert heard didn't tell Robert his father was going to whop his ass. The water splattered in his father's face, leaving him shaking like a wet dog. When Robert's father finally caught his breath, he told his son, "Go in the house. I'll be in there in a few minutes."

Robert ran into the house like a little puppy with his tail between his legs. When his father was finished washing his car, Robert jumped into bed and lay as though he was asleep. Unfortunately, his father didn't have any respect for sleeping at the time. He whopped Robert like he was in Robert's dreams as the big bad wolf being his worst nightmare.

On a few occasions, when Robert and his sister would stop over at their father's house to see how he was doing, he would just crack the door open and peep out and say he was busy and that they should drop by later. Janet didn't like any of his kids or his family. Janet did socialize with Robert from time to time—not that she cared more for Robert than for Robert's sisters. She just knew Robert wasn't going out of his way to kiss her ass.

And for years, Robert and his sister decided that it was better to just step out of their father's life so he could keep the peace with his wife. After a few years had passed, when Robert's father's car had seen its better days and he couldn't afford to buy another one since he was on a fixed income, Robert called his father and told him he was picking him up the next morning to buy him another car.

The very next morning, upon their arrival at the car lot, his father picked out the car he wanted. As he was test-driving the vehicle he wanted, Robert glanced out of the corner of his eyes and noticed the tears running down his father's face. Robert didn't let on to his father that he had seen him crying over his son's kindness.

Robert's kindness brought his father back in the shadows of his past from the tears running down his face. The tears were a reflection of the pureness of his heart that showed the words he had kept bottled up within for years. The time Robert's father wanted Robert to pay him to co-sign for him a car, but this time, no co-signer was needed, just a signature of Robert's heart.

Just the thought of Robert loving him despite what they had been through, the times Robert knocked on his door and was turned away. Robert knew it was time to turn the page to a different chapter.

Robert's thoughts drifted to his father, their ups and their downs. He kept a roof over Robert's head and cared for him when he couldn't care for himself.

When he was a child, his father held him up and held his hands and walked beside him when he made his very first step to keep him from falling. *Today, today, Daddy, I am here to hold your hand and to keep you from falling. It doesn't matter where we've been. What's more important is where we are going. This day, this day is the love we both had kept bottled up within. And no matter what, you, sir—you, sir, are still my father.*

In all of Robert's life, he never felt the love he felt right then from his father just by seeing his father's tears. Robert wouldn't have traded that moment for all the money in the world. Love surely was priceless.

And Robert knew it wasn't about the car he was buying his father—it was the love his father had kept in the shadows of his heart. His cup had runneth over.

And from that day on, he wasn't only a father but Robert's best friend. They could actually feel each other's heart, and Robert's mind continued to drift. He remembered how Janet, his father's wife, had called him and told him his father was sick. Robert had flown into New Orleans to go see about his father. When he entered the room, he heard his father praying. He didn't even know Robert was there, and he hardly remembered anything.

But what was so amazing was when he heard his father praying. A man of God (minister) who had Alzheimer's hardly remembering anything, but prayer was imprinted in his mind, his heart, and his soul; and the name *Jesus* was still in his spirit. Robert walked close to his bed and looked down at him and said, "Daddy, it's your son." He continued praying, blocking out everything that surrounded him.

Janet said, "He doesn't remember anything." Right at that moment, she walked over to the bed and shook him. "Honey, it's your son."

Robert's father stopped praying and said these very words: "Oh, my son, whom I love very much . . ." And he went back to just praying and praising the Lord. Robert had never in his life seen a man—no man—pray like his father did, not even in the state of mind he was in. The name *Jesus* was still imprinted in his mind and in the prayer words that flowed out of his mouth . . .

Robert could remember one time his wife told him how his father was losing weight and that she believed he had cancer. Robert's father was examined by a physician, who didn't find any signs of cancer. Robert then received a phone call from his auntie that troubled his heart. He didn't realize what was going on with his father until his auntie called him and said his wife was starving him to death and didn't want anyone to feed him.

Janet had totally brainwashed Robert's father, told him he was too big and needed to lose weight. He had lost so much weight until he was too weak and ended up bedridden. In fact, his father didn't weigh any more than 105 pounds when he died.

Robert's auntie had said a friend, who was also a friend of Janet's, told her of how Janet had called her to come sit with Robert's father while she went on an errand and she had to sneak Robert's father some food, because his wife refused to feed him. Robert immediately asked his auntie, would her friend be willing to testify to what his father's wife was doing to him? Robert told his auntie he was coming to New Orleans to get a court order to remove his father from his wife's custody. *Hold on, Daddy. I am coming to get you.* But sad to say, the very next day, Robert's father was dead,

On the day of Robert's father's funeral, Janet had published the obituary, where none of his kids was mentioned. Robert's father had been married to Satan himself. And about eleven months later, the year 1999, Robert lost his mother too. After Robert had been called out on an assignment, he received a call from his sister Keisha. Keisha informed him their mother had been admitted on one of her follow-up visits to her doctor. He was very concerned about his mother and called her at the hospital. Did she need him to come home to see her? Her exact words were, "I am all right. It would be different if I was really sick, and you don't need to leave your job." And not knowing he wouldn't hear her voice again.

The very next day, his sister Keisha called him and said their mother's condition had turned for the worse, and that she was in a coma. Keisha was going to nursing school out of town at the time and had to go back to take her nursing exam. Without hesitation, he caught a flight home to Peoria, beating himself up with guilt. He felt guilty not going to see her when his sister first called. Upon his arrival at the hospital in Chicago, tears in his eyes, his mother was still in a coma.

The sadness penetrated his heart, and he prayed to God not to take his mother. It was another dark day in his life; he fasted and prayed to God to hear his cry. *Lord, please don't take my mother—the woman who prayed for me when I didn't pray for myself. As a mother, she fought a good fight of caring and going without for me to have what I needed.*

She was a woman who gave him her last from the reflection of her heart. She endured with all his good and his bad and took care of him when he was sick. The woman who walked through the house making sure he was under the covers and safe from the draft seeping in through the windows from the bitter cold, making sure he was warm. The woman who encouraged him to be strong when he thought there was no hope. *Lord, how can I tell her to forgive me for not being there when she needed me the most?* A short time later, her sister Alice arrived in Chicago from out of town.

Robert went into the room with Aunt Alice. "Ma dear," he said, "look at who's here to see you."

His mother opened her eyes for a second, as though she was aware of their presence.

Her sister prayed out loud to God. *Please, Lord, don't take my sister.* In all the days of his life, Robert never felt as he did looking down at his mother, not knowing if he would ever hear her voice again.

The things he had never told her, the things he wanted to say. The flowers he never gave her that he wanted to give. For a moment, Robert went into a deep trance, remembering an old saying: "We should always be careful of the things we say to anyone, because the last thing we say may be the last thing they hear. We can love so much but still so little. Expressing your love is very precious, because with death, there's no coming back."

The doctor came out and said that a large percentage of her liver was gone, that she wasn't going to make it. The next day, Robert was in the room when his mother took her very last breath. Robert immediately told the family not to call Keiska to tell her their mother had passed, he wanted her to be able to concentrate on taking her exam at school, since she was returning home the next day. All that was on his mind were the things he could have done for her while she was alive, and didn't. He would live with the hurt for the rest of his life—not giving her flowers while she was still alive, not calling her every day just to say, "Ma dear, I love you."

Just the simple things he could have done. The little money he had given her was nothing compared to the things he could have done or the things he could have said. For many years after, grief over his mother filled his heart, and he couldn't hold back the tears that flowed down his face. It was as though a water faucet had been opened and he couldn't turn it off. And all he could say in his mind was, *I love you, ma dear.* Robert's mind drifted, tears will soon vanish but the mind and heart will always be filled with memories.

Keisha was still in school, and he knew his mother would want him to make sure she finished school. And it was the least he could do to carry out his mother's greatest wish. He and his other sister gave Keisha everything their mother left behind, even the remainder of their mother's insurance money, for her to finish school.

The attorney they had hired told them he had never seen family members signing over their inheritance to another member without any confrontation. They all wanted their mother's dream to come true. And the material things she had left behind were nothing compared to what they had lost when they lost her.

After the funeral, Robert knew life would still go on, and now he had a wife and his kids to take care of. He had to get away to help keep his mind off his mother. He had so much bottled up within him he could hardly catch his breath. He thought going on another assignment for a couple of months would ease his pain, but in his silent moments, he found himself bursting into tears, hiding his emotions from the others; but he realized God did things for a reason, and that being born was a part of death, and death was a part of life. But still, when he had moments to himself, he couldn't stop the tears that ran down his face.

Robert's mind drifted all the way back to his childhood, when his father and his mother would have him and his sisters and other saints of the church on their knees at the altar in church tarrying for the Holy Ghost. When the Spirit of God came in, many of the saints and Robert's sisters would start to shout and turn over chairs and move many benches. Robert still stayed in his same stance, not feeling anything. On many occasions, his father kept him at the altar tarrying for the Holy Ghost. Still, Robert stayed in the same mood, not feeling anything. Robert's mind would drift in so many directions, not allowing the Holy Spirit to come in. His mind wasn't focused on God.

One day Robert's father came to him in anger. "Why is it everyone else can feel God's presence but not you?" And Robert replied in a soft, respectful manner, "Daddy, I am not going to church playing with God, turning over chairs and moving benches when I don't feel anything. I can't play with God like that." But still, on the first Sunday of every month, Robert would still take communion, not really understanding what communion really meant. All he knew was that he loved the Welch grape juice and the cracker that was served. Robert never listened to the words, what communion stood for. He couldn't wait to get in line to get that good-tasting juice and to bite down on that piece of cracker.

Until one day he listened to the words.

> Wherefore whosoever shall eat this bread. And drink this cup of the Lord, unworthy, shall be guilty of the body and the blood of the Lord. But let a man examine himself, and so let him eat of that bread, and drink of that cup.
>
> For he eateth and drinketh unworthily, eateth and drinketh damnation to himself, not discerning the Lord's body.
>
> For this cause many are weak and sickly among you, and many sleep. (1 Cor. 11:27–30)

The word *sleep* had an impact on Robert. He did not want to be the cause of the death of a loved one. In his mind, let every man examine himself.

And from that point on, even until this day, Robert refused to take communion. If anything about him was not according to the Word of God, he wanted to avoid damnation on himself or others.

And what was so amazing was that a few years before his passing, Robert's father brought him back to his childhood. He said, "Son, I remember when I got angry with you for not feeling the Spirit of God when you were a little boy tarrying for the Holy Ghost. And you replied, 'Daddy, I can't play with God.'"

CHAPTER 7

Coat of Many Colors

AT HOME TOGETHER ON A Sunday after Robert had been away for a couple months, Mary brought up the subject of going to church. He was feeling exhausted after being away at work, working twelve hours a day and seven days a week for over sixty days. He told her she could go, but he just wanted to relax because he was feeling so drained.

He thought he had said a curse word. Her attitude exposed with arrogance; it was though he had let Satan out the gate. She braced up to him, breathing raggedly, as though she was ready to fight. Her whole character turned with many different colors. She was so outraged, screaming and stomping her feet. It was like looking through clear shallow waters; Robert began to see right through her. She seemed as though she wanted to be a freak in the bedroom and wanted him to be a child in a classroom, raising a hand for permission to speak. Her camouflaged gold-plated heart had begun to tarnish and fade.

He stood quietly for a moment, looking in her eyes, replying with a sharpness in his voice, "I don't believe in fighting. When it comes to fighting and playing with knives and guns, we don't need to be together. It's time to go." He added, "I am not your child but your husband. You need to talk to your kids in such a manner."

When his mother died, she had come out of the closet, as if to say, *Who's going to have your back now?*

She had so much bitterness trapped within she was like a time bomb waiting to go off. The way she lashed out and braced up to him, like she was provoking him to hit her. He could see she was primed and straining, ready for combat and violence, which must have been a staple from her previous relationships. She herself was still living in the shadows of her past.

Mary's hostile attitude left Robert in total shock, pushing him farther away, and the little love he had started to feel for her tiptoed out the back door.

Robert could only shake his head. He didn't believe what had happened. All he could think of was how she did a good job of putting her best foot forward. He chuckled, saying to himself, *The girl should have been an actor.* She left home wearing her Sunday best and returned home as though nothing had happened, and she had been baptized again and had shed her skin like a snake.

He wanted out of the marriage, but he kept his kids in mind. He was willing to sacrifice his happiness for the kids' well-being. Now he had to play a role—an actor hiding his true feelings with a smile.

He felt it would be easier for him to pay her than to be her lover or her husband. On his short stay there with his kids before being called out on another assignment, she brought up her car in their conversation.

He knew her car wasn't in the best condition. She went to try to trade it for a new one, but with her credit, the dealer turned her down. Feeling as though he was in her debt for taking care of his kids, he purchased her a brand-new car to make sure she and the kids had good transportation before he left again.

In the back of his mind, he thought he was giving her material things to ease his conscience to keep himself from feeling he was using her to take care of his kids. Right after he had purchased the car, his job called him to go on another assignment.

Leaving his kids the second time was much easier, knowing they had adjusted a little to their new home. They understood his motive for leaving them again with Mary. But after his fight with her, they were still in a state of shock. He didn't regret leaving her, but he knew he would miss his kids.

Keeping his distance from her seemed to improve their bond, allowing him to escape from having any sexual contact. Playing his role as a husband was much easier from a distance than in person. Their long-distance relationship gave him the reinforcement to ignore her hostile actions, and to think only of the kids.

He thought he had a beautiful wife from a distance, but she was a tiger in the bedroom with sharp paws, ready to claw his eyes out. Suddenly he couldn't understand all the good things she did, how she let her bad overweigh her good. From a distance, she was the perfect wife. She gave her all to her marriage and to his kids, but sleeping under the same roof with her, hostility invaded their relationship. Observing her in his short stay home, he could see she was a nagging mother with her own kids, which pushed them to leave home at an early age. Her kids loved their mother and were used to her ways, but still, they got along with her better from a distance.

So staying under the same roof with her was definitely out of the question. And he wondered, would he follow in her kids' steps?

In his conversations with her over the phone, he had an image of her as the perfect wife—a passionate wife filled with so much understanding. Verbally, her convincing words and her passion for his kids gave him hope, but still, he was having a hard time trying to find love for her in their marriage.

Each day she was his monitor, giving him an update on the kids and how well they were doing; and for that reason, she was like a magnet that pulled him closer to her, making him feel he would be forever in her debt, willing to put up with all of her moods, and even her faults.

And her helping his baby daughter Nora with her homework was a big improvement from where she had started. He couldn't have done this without her help, a realization that left him with a passion and gratitude for having her in his life, and no matter what, he wouldn't ever leave her for another woman. He would try to love her in every way he could, even if it was from a distance.

He knew he had to prepare himself for the worst and be willing to take care of her, like she was taking care of his kids, for better or for worse.

Even from a distance, she tried to take care of him as well. Anything he needed while at work, it was first priority for her; she was intent on taking care of her husband. He was so amazed at how important she made him feel.

Every day while he was away, she never worried him about herself or the kids. She was totally in control. She told him about how she really loved the house she was renting, and that she wouldn't mind trying to buy it. She called it her little dollhouse. He told her that when he got home, he would inquire about the house, ask her landlady about possibly buying it for her.

After the end of another assignment, he called her to give her his flight schedule so she could pick him up from the airport. He found her waiting patiently, reading a book by the baggage claim. When they got home, the kids were still in school. By the time they entered the bedroom just a moment later, she had stripped out of her clothes, hornier than ever.

The more sex he gave her, the more she wanted as she gasped for breath. She told him she just loved the way he made love to her. He knew he had to satisfy her, because he didn't want her to catch on that he had no desire to do so. Having sex with her was like planting evil thoughts in her mind, not wanting a fly to light on him with a touch of jealousy, wanting him all to herself, and everyone else she wanted to stay at a distance, even his kids.

He was so anxious for the kids to come home from school, knowing they would be surprised to see him.

During the time he spent with her, the room was filled with her smiles. When the kids got home, they were so overwhelmed. They didn't want to leave his bedroom; they just wanted to talk and be in his presence.

He noticed his wife had many smiles. But he felt a sensation of jealousy with regard to his oldest daughter. She had good things to say about his younger daughter, but she painted a different picture about the older one, saying she was a liar, and she hated a liar, forgetting she had lied to him about paying a phone bill when she didn't. She was subjecting him to double standards, lying to get what she wanted but hating being lied to.

She led him to believe she was trying to put a wall between him and his older daughter after seeing how close they were. He really did enjoy his kids, and besides, his kids were the only family he had there; the rest were living in different states, and his only communication with them was by phone. He even noticed that when he talked to his relatives on the home phone in her presence, she would glance at him with a suspicious look. And even when he was on his cell phone, she acted as though it disturbed her.

It didn't take long for Satan to come out of the cage. She snapped, And you, sitting in my bedroom talking to all those womans. She wouldn't say *women*. And she told him about how he and the kids were in the bedroom talking, and how they would stop talking when she entered the bedroom, as though he and the kids were talking about her. Her accusation was an outrage, but he chose not to engage her. She took a hammer and smashed his cell phone.

Robert had been home only one day, and already her nagging made him as though he was in the bedroom with a total stranger. He knew her only from a distance as his meek and humble wife. This woman had so many different personalities, and moments later, she would act like nothing even happened. She would be laughing with joy, standing on the bed, jumping up and down, laughing with a loud and squeaky voice. Her true personality was beginning to show, and the kids would just look at him and at each other in silence. It was as though they wanted to say, *Daddy, where in the world did you find this one?*

He wasn't worried about her mistreating the kids; she knew the kids were her security to keep him with her. He was thinking it was time for him to go, hoping the phone would ring for him to go on another assignment, knowing it was impossible for him to live under the same roof with her.

It didn't bother him too much knowing he wouldn't be there too long. He managed to talk to her landlady regarding buying the house for her. The landlady told him she was willing to do a contract for the deed if he put $5,000 down. Robert agreed to do so.

Robert's job called him again on another assignment. He told her landlady he was leaving the very next day and that he would give her the down payment when he returned. The landlady agreed to sell the house on his return home.

Still, Robert was willing to sacrifice his happiness for the kids, although at the thought of living with Mary, he was totally miserable. He couldn't wait to go to bed early, hoping the time would pass for him to leave for the airport to catch his flight the next morning.

The night before his flight, he pretended to be sleepy, hoping he could escape from making love to her, hiding his lack of desire to do so.

He just wanted to keep his distance; even looking at her from a distance with binoculars was too close for comfort. Her erratic behavior left him always holding his guard up, not knowing what to expect next. Slowly but surely, he realized her elevator wasn't going all the way up to the top floor. The woman was really crazy.

But she was fully aware of doing the things she wanted to do and had a lot of street sense to beat the system, and she knew how to get things done. She had different faces to fit her lifestyle, to do the things she wanted to do with no guilt.

To her, being religious was like clay, molding it to her own lifestyle, giving her permission to step out of the guideline of her religious beliefs. Her mouth spoke it, but her heart was so far way. When he showed her he disapproved and reminded her she was supposed to have been saved and in church, she would reply, "Things are different, and we are now in modern times."

He would reply, "The Bible has been the same as long as I can remember, and the Bible never has changed. But people do."

But she was always drowning out other people, ready to preach to them if something wasn't beneficial to her.

But Robert found himself feeling sorry for her, picking up her slack. He was being her guardian angel, with his mind made up to take care of her, like she was taking care of his kids. He was trapped with a woman carrying the title of his wife, wondering if she was going to be his worst nightmare. Robert reassured himself that he had his kids' best interest at heart, which put him in total denial of her behavior.

Upon his departure the next morning, he braced himself for a farewell of hugging and kissing, with no room to fantasize, which left him less energetic to be in her presence. She was his wife, but only from a distance.

In a moment of silence, he found himself trying to analyze her different personalities. What was causing her to explode when she did so much good? He loved the things she did from a distance, but he hated to be in her presence. Yet despite all her faults, he wanted to love her—not for the things she did for the kids but for playing her part as his wife, for them being a mother and a father picking up each other's slack.

After his assignment had ended once again, he was anxious to go home to be with his kids and his wife. This time he hoped things in their relationship would be a little different, without any confrontation that would push him out the door again.

Upon his arrival back in Peoria, she was in her same composure and routine, waiting patiently by the baggage claim for her husband, in the heat of passion that would lead him to the bedroom. Making love to her wasn't as hard the first time, but after being with her awhile, he realized again that there was no spark in their romance.

She beguiled people and friends he knew with her own personal convictions. She told him how the devil would tempt her at times to go and find someone to make love to her, and how no one would ever know. Robert's mind drifted with this thought, a saved and sanctified woman with a lust of adultery in her heart. If it crossed her mind to cheat on God, then what there's to stop her from cheating on him. Then she would go on to tell him about how she used to be a two-timer, a three-timer, even a four-timer, cheating with different men at the same time. She was living in her past, in the gutters that went beyond his imagination of the dirt that soiled her mind, which turned out to be no illusion.

She spoke boldly, to a point of letting her dirty laundry air out. She bragged of her reputation, about the different men she had slept with. And she was proud to tell him her bedtime stories from the past.

Robert didn't want to hurt her feelings, so he kept his thoughts to himself: *In other words, you were a whore.* She laughed over how she had cheated, and how her family gave her the nickname Undercover. He chuckled. What man wanted to hear about his wife being a whore?

After listening to her making such a statement, he finally understood why his phone conversations drove her to a state of suspicion of reaping what she had sown. She was bringing out the skeletons in her closet. Robert knew that trying to build a relationship with no foundation gave them no hope for the future. Not with her judging him for what she had done in her past, now leaving an imprint in her mind, thinking he was going to do the same to her. Just for a moment, Robert went into a trance. If she was living in the shadows of her past, her past would always be her future.

Robert was aware of the skeletons in his own closet. He had done his share of cheating and lying, which had left him with shame, but he had asked God for forgiveness. He had even gone to his first wife and asked her for forgiveness for the affairs he had during their marriage. Shaking the dust from his feet wasn't a subject to brag about.

He held his head up and kept in mind what the Bible said. "Let those among you with no sin cast the first stone." He wondered how she could criticize anyone with the skeletons still hanging in her closet. Her past was her worst enemy.

While on his assignment, she had gone to the extreme of retrieving his password for his pager to keep track of all his messages. Her overwhelming suspicion was like a sharp knife waiting to rip their relationship apart. Never in his life had he met anyone so evil-minded. She was eaten up by jealousy and a tendency toward destruction, wanting to keep him away from all females, even his relatives and his daughters.

Still, it never crossed his mind that she was jealous of him even holding a phone conversation with his relatives and his own daughters until eight years later.

He never thought she would be ridiculous. She always would say she heard him over the phone talking to all those women in the bedroom, disrespecting her. Still, it never dawned on him that she was speaking of his relatives.

What she was saying was puzzling to him; it just didn't make sense. He asked himself, what reason would he have to talk to another female in her presence and disrespect her in such a manner? Just being in her presence was always an occasion for nagging and getting in the midst of her argumentative attitude.

Keeping his promise, he made an attempt to purchase the house she called her little dollhouse. The landlady was a little hesitant, putting him off until later. But the strangest thing was that the landlady didn't take his down payment of $5,000, and she discontinued their rent. Robert thought she might still be working on the paperwork for the contract for the deed.

He couldn't help but feel he was still in his wife's debt for taking care of his kids; and in her own little way, she would remind him of that debt by telling him she wanted this or that, as though to say, *You owe me that much in terms of restitution.*

Her greedy side was slowly but surely beginning to surface. His positive thinking of wanting his kids to be happy left him clueless as to her motive, using his kids as bait with an invisible hook. She invested in the kids, buying them things they needed, and she never once asked him for a dime; but her kind ways just didn't match her attitude.

He observed her nagging her own kids time and time again, watching her kids keeping their distance from her. He started to realize that nagging was in her nature, and he decided to try to get along with her with a different scenario.

His first approach was to let her know she didn't have to worry about him leaving her for another woman, because her actions and behavior over him talking to his daughters or his relatives showed signs of her being insecure. He was living for the future, and she was still living in her past. He attempted to pamper her, but to her, it was a sign of guilt.

She snapped, "And you must be out of your rabbit-ass mind." She told him, "You want me to just sit here while you talk to other women."

Her reaction threw him completely off course. He had said to her, "If you let me talk to other women, I will never leave you." He regretted not following his instincts not to marry her.

Her cheating with so many different men was a reflection of her past, what she used to do, and she was intent on refusing to let him do the same things she did.

Repeatedly, she reminded him, laughing wickedly, of the nicknames given to her by her family: *FBI* and *Undercover.* The nickname *Undercover* only made Robert's mind drift. How many men's beds was she in under the covers? And the day he married her, he would have been better off going shopping at Walmart. Filled with frustration time and time again, listening to her bedtime stories, he said, "You were just a whore, and maybe you still are."

He was still trying to isolate her past. His life now was all about his kids, and he just wanted to settle down. He sought employment in many different places, trying to be near her and his kids. Giving her material things for the well-being of his kids didn't mean anything at all to him. Buying her a car meant giving his kids good transportation to get from point A to B, and even buying a house was putting a roof not only over her head but his kids' as well.

For his kids' sake, Robert put up with Mary's moods, her nagging, and her tormented yelling and her hanging up the phone while he was holding a conversation with his relatives. Once, he had lashed out at her, telling her the only thing holding their marriage together was his job, because he was not home long enough to seek a divorce and make other preparations for the kids.

He knew he would have divorce her the very first few months of their marriage if it had not been for his kids and his job. Because he was never home long enough to address the situation, at most he would only be home with her about seven days out of every two or three months, being with her at most forty-two days out of a year.

Being at home with her seven days every two months was like being incarcerated the entire time, making his stay with her seem like six months. He was totally miserable being her husband. Still, he made every attempt to make her happy.

After Mary's landlady took so long to make her decision to sell the house, Robert decided to build a house for them from the ground up. She told him she was tired of Peoria, and they agreed to build a house in Mississippi. And he thought they were going to have a better relationship living elsewhere, and it would help her to put her past behind her. He was wishing his mother could have came with them because of her age and because she needed to get out of the snow and the bitter coldness of the weather in Chicago. Mississippi was a place he wanted to live, and his mother wanted to move there too, to be close to her young sister.

Mary, being very supportive, allowed him to save over $30,000 in a matter of a few months, and they purchased over an acre of land to build their home on. Still, he had no knowledge she was a time bomb waiting to go off to proclaim their marital possessions, not knowing her support came with a price. Because she knew that the more they accomplished in this marriage, the more she could take.

Mary's reactions were like being born all over again. A person with a sense of direction with a goal, still his eyes were open, and yet so blind to see the woman he married was filled with greed, building up their marital assets to take control, and being able to control him, buying time for his retirement as well.

She slowly showed a different personality with a lot of charm. Her main subject was her husband, her Romeo, taking her out of the ghetto into another world she had never experienced before. Robert's older daughter Tasha appeared to be able to see right through her camouflage to the coldness of her heart, how she was playing a role for personal gain. Mary never had anything good to say about Tasha, always calling her a liar. Still, Tasha respected her, because that was what her father had taught her to do, to respect her elders.

He instantly put their yesterdays behind him, because the past had no value. Having peace in his marriage and their home meant more than money, silver, or gold. Her smile and her attitude put a different fragrance in the air that motivated him to give her his all. Nothing in this world he wouldn't have done for her. It was his way of appreciating her for taking care of his kids.

Still, his eyes were open, but he was too blind to see his baby daughter was frightened of her stepmother. Nora would jump with fear just hearing Mary's name. She was terrified of isolating her silence with fear, afraid to speak out, knowing her dad was there only for a few days, and Mary was like her shadow that would still be around. She was like a scarecrow in the middle of a cornfield that had the kids frightened to look at her from all angles.

Robert was too wrapped up trying to pay his debt to Mary and too blind to see the kids were trapped in a house of horror with their stepmom, which made them play as doubles of Cinderella.

CHAPTER 8

The First Divorce Attempt with The First Attorney

S TILL, ROBERT WAS IN DENIAL of the state of his relationship with Mary and still hoping to feel love for her, which was like trying to blend water with oil, both of which would always be separate, owing their difference in texture. With less hesitation, he put their plans together, drawing up the blueprint for their home, going to different bookstores to look at different home designs.

After they had done the precise design for their home, Robert went to Louisiana, where he had an architect draw up the blueprint. Mary was drowning in the sensation of having a home. She had never had one of her own before, and of her own design, which she did on her own, to perfection. Upon submitting his plans to the bank, Robert didn't put her name on the loan, with her credit being bad and knowing the bank would turn him down for the loan.

The bank requested a copy of the blueprint along with the loan application. The bank approved his loan for much more than what he needed to put up the house. And keeping Mary in an upbeat mood, there was less of a chance for confusion.

She was very excited about the whole process of getting a home built, and it was giving her the security of being a stockholder, legally binding him and giving her more collateral on him so he wouldn't ever leave her; and if he did, he would pay the price. Her mind was filled with greed and an extraordinary polished-up attitude of being very supportive.

Robert transformed himself and tossed all his fears aside, and refused to let anything keep him from playing his role as a husband and a father, because he had his family's best interests at heart. In his mind, he knew there was a time to be born and a time to die, and he wanted to separate himself from the negative things that would poison his mind and to live each day as though it was his last.

He sought employment with the sheriff's department in Mississippi, where their home was to be built. And a short time later, he was hired at the sheriff's department, which allowed him to finish all the paperwork for the bank that the underwriter wanted him to complete.

He left Peoria alone, leaving his wife and kids for the meantime. It didn't matter to Mary that he was leaving, because he was going to achieve their goal of putting up their new home.

After staying in Mississippi a while, Robert started to feel concerned about the mobile homes in the area, bringing down the value of their home. It was like putting up a $200,000 home near a junkyard. And if they ever decided to sell it, they would never get their money's worth out of it.

Still, he went through the motion of having the house built after the bank had appraised the land he had bought and given their approval. Still uncertain about building their home there, he waited until the last minute before construction started, changing his mind not to build where they would be surrounded by mobile homes.

He told Mary he had changed his mind, that he was looking for a better area to build. He gave the sheriff's department two weeks' notice before returning to Peoria and to his old job. He ended up selling the land for what he had purchased it. Upon his return, his old job called him on an assignment after he had been gone for approximately three months.

His plans were still in place, but with a different scenario as to where their home was to be built. His mind drifted as he tried to find the perfect piece of land, exploring other places in different parts of Mississippi.

She seemed mollified by his explanation and was being supportive. The lack of confusion and fighting helped to calm his thoughts. He just wanted her and the kids to have the best. He decided to take her on a trip to Mississippi to explore other options for them to build their home.

He observed the shift in her attitude, how she did not seem to be intimidated by other females who would normally pose a threat to their relationship as long as her mind didn't have time to idle. He chuckled at a funny thought, hoping nothing would pinch her trigger and bring her back to her old self and activate her negative thoughts.

She showed perfection in being a wife, helping them to reach their expectation of being a family and showing a reflection of teamwork. She didn't seem to have camouflages as she beguiled him into seeing her as the perfect wife, playing a role to get what she wanted. Still, he didn't detect a flaw in their marriage that was built on material things fueled by her greed.

His oversight of her sense of greed gave him less complication of having any thoughts of the material things they gained, which would be a level tool for her to fight him in court. She was being very calm and patient with the things he accomplished today, which would be the rope she would use to hang him tomorrow.

She seemed amazed by his ability to get things done.

Her brother told him how she would brag about how smart he was. Robert did not know Mary felt all she needed to do was follow his lead and the material things in their marriage would legally bind them, and she would take control, if he ever decided to go in a different direction. Her plans were well beyond his imagination.

As time passed, and they were still looking for the perfect piece of land, they explored some new construction homes, but none was to her taste. She was very picky. Exploring more land, they came across this new home that was designed somewhat like the blueprint of the house they wanted to build. Mary really loved this house, and seeing the delight on her face, he knew their search was over.

Robert submitted all the information on the home to the bank, and then they waited for the construction of the house to finish. Meanwhile, until they were ready to move into their home, they let his sister, who lived in Atlanta, to move into the house, and his daughter Tasha was moving into the house with his sister.

For some reason, Mary was still jealous of the relationship he had with Tasha. Mary was still taking care of her mother, and they still needed to decide who would take care of her if Mary moved to Mississippi. After all, it was Mary's income taking care of her mother, and she always kept saying how much she loved her job and taking care of her mother.

Robert was glad she was able to work at home, because she had a condition in her head and her face. When the weather changed, sure as rain, snow, or dark clouds, she would be in so much pain; and at times, one side of her face would swell. His heart went out to her, and no matter what, after finding out her sickness, Robert decided he was there to stay.

She had a CAT scan done, which revealed she might have an old wound on one side of her brain. At once, Robert's mind drifted back to what her brother had told him about how she and her ex-husband fought and how he would punch her on the side of her head.

Her mother was bedfast, and on a couple of occasions, he would mention to her that she shouldn't leave her mother home alone while she went to church. On one occasion, he was in his bedroom, and after a while, he went to her mother's bedroom to check on her, and found her unconscious from lack of oxygen. He called for the paramedics and her mother was rushed to the hospital. His heart ached for her mother and her well-being. He treated her mother like she was his own. He missed his mother so much, and when he looked at Mary's mother, he saw his own.

Their plan was to move into their home in about a year or more, after making plans of him seeking employment in Peoria.

Mary agreed to let Robert's sister move into their home until all their plans in Peoria were finalized. In fact, she was overjoyed to let his sister move into their new home. As months passed, Mary's plan was to let her mother move in with one of her sisters when the time came for them to move into their home. Slowly but surely, they set their mind on moving into their new home in Mississippi.

His mind was on her mother, not wanting to leave her behind. He totally ignored something his daughter Tasha had told him. Mary had said to his daughter, "Your daddy better not ever leave me." Her evil thoughts started to show, how the gain of material things was at the root of her marriage, which gave her a contract of security.

Still ignoring his distasteful thoughts about her, he never stopped providing and trying to give his all to her and his kids. Leaving her wasn't on his agenda, and another woman wasn't on his menu. What he carried was the righteousness in his heart for her, and accepting her bad and good and their vows for better or for worse. The material things were all she had in mind; little did she know he would give them to her without a fight.

He knew the things she put on a silver platter was plentiful, if she really believed in the God she claimed she served, he would grant her anything her heart desire. Gradually but surely, Robert started to realize this marriage just wasn't going to work. After the house was built and the closing was finalized, she went back to her old self, to her outrage and trying to provoke him to hit her—something that wasn't in his character. He would just chuckle, thinking, *Who let Satan out of his cage?*

Instead he still felt he owed her a debt for taking care of his kids, for which he compensated her by buying her a new car, still wanting her to have the best because, after all, she was his wife. He started to realize that the more he gave, the more she wanted, and the more she ridiculed him. It was just as the old saying goes: "A leopard will never change his spots."

Going into the same old routine with her, he started to get frustrated. And what he hated the most was how she would try to provoke him to hit her, as though she was trying to set him up to get thrown into jail. The more love he showed, the bigger the stones she would throw.

Now he was filled with so much anger. He just wanted to get out of his marriage; he felt incarcerated in his own home. At times, he wasn't even worried about what she would take from him. He was willing to give her what she was entitled to with regard to their marital assets. He thought the longer he stayed in this marriage with her, the deeper he would sink, because it was in her nature to be filled with greed.

After being married for only about four years, he decided to find an attorney and put some money down for the filing of his divorce and the attorney's fees.

The attorney's secretary informed him the divorce would be cheaper if Mary would sign and not contest it. He didn't tell Mary he had gone to an attorney to seek advice on filing a divorce. He just hinted around, testing the waters, and asked her what she would want if they got a divorce. She never could give him an answer. It was as though she was saying, *You will find that out when the time comes.*

The attorney he went to made him angry. He was not able to talk to the attorney in person. His secretary would always say she would give him the message, which really made Robert very uncomfortable. Hiring this attorney was like throwing money down the drain. He realized this attorney wasn't what he was looking for.

To help distance himself from Mary and keep his mind occupied, Robert decided to start his own lawn care business. Mary showed great support for him starting his own business and did whatever she could to help him. His greatest task was to get certified by the Department of Transportation while seeking big contracts. He went the whole nine yards to get his business incorporated, among many other things, to meet their requirements. And he purchased a lot of lawn care equipment.

In other words, the situation—that is being employed and trying to keep up with his own business—was beginning to overwhelm him. But Mary's mind was flooded with greed. And him having his own business gave her a vision of a dollar sign. Her devilish thoughts never missed a beat.

CHAPTER 9

The Death of Mary's Mother and the Second Divorce Attempt with The Second Attorney

A VERY SHORT TIME AFTER ROBERT was called on another assignment, he didn't know that it would be the last time he would see the woman he had treated as his mother alive. After he had been away for a few weeks, he received a phone call from Mary's daughter informing him her grandmother was dead. He felt as though he was going through a repeat of his mother's death.

He left his job to support his wife and be with her during her time of grief. Upon his arrival, he learned that Mary's mother had been left alone again and had died from lack of oxygen. No one knew what had happened to her oxygen machine. It appeared she had tried to call Mary on the phone at church, but she didn't get through.

Robert's mind drifted to him telling Mary not to leave her mother alone after the last incident that almost ended her life from lack of oxygen. He had been there with her mother the first time it happened, and he called the paramedics and saved her life. After that, he asked her not to leave her home alone again. Mary had gotten so comfortable leaving her mother alone so many times, ignoring what he had asked of her, and now her disobedience had cost her mother's life.

Robert was so angry with Mary, but now wasn't the right time to show his anger, nor was it the right place. She had enough guilt to deal with having disobeyed him about not leaving her mother alone. What was most devastating was that her mother was bedfast and couldn't do anything for herself. After her mother's death, the whole family was in an uproar about the insurance money—who was getting what and who was trying to get over getting the most.

Robert was very sad to see Mary's mother buried and gone, and her kids were filled with so much greed. After the funeral, Robert and Mary had more freedom to relocate and to make arrangements to move into their home. Robert started buying furniture to furnish their home, using his own money, but her family claimed she used her mother's insurance policy to buy the furniture for their new house. The whole family seemed as though they were brainless and their love for one another had perished.

After the death of Mary's mother, Robert didn't pressure Mary to work because of her condition—which he had no knowledge of before they were married. He had more of a load to carry picking up her debts and keeping them afloat. They were preparing to move, and their plans were to move in June.

Before Mary's mother passed, Robert had been looking for a job in Peoria for many years. A few months before June, an unexpected thing happened: the company he was applying for a job with called him. He couldn't believe it. Right when he was making plans to leave, the job he was seeking called him, turning him in a whole different direction from leaving Peoria.

Mary's attitude was becoming unbearable, and the house they bought wasn't theirs anymore but hers. She had changed the ownership of their home from plural to singular, not realizing the house belonged to the bank.

Robert asked her to be patient. He couldn't just leave his job after having just been hired and carrying their load, going to Mississippi, not knowing how he was going to pay their debts, and hers as well. According to the law, her debts were his debts as well. A short time after, she insisted she was moving into her house in Mississippi, whether or not he came with her. He pleaded with her to wait, that when the time was right, they would move there together. Her sense of greed had sabotaged their financial ability to deal with the obstacles that stood before them.

He refused to let her dictate and overrule his decision when he knew the load he had to bear, without any help from her. Things got devastating for him each month. He would pay a credit card and turn around and use the payment he made to buy grocery.

Mary's daughter Tammy was pregnant at the time, and Robert asked her to stay, because she needed Mary the most. And he asked her not to uproot his sister from their home in Mississippi, knowing he wasn't ready to make that move yet, and his sister Sally was making the house payments each month. Mary showed no pity about uprooting his sister, but she put the guilt on his shoulder to bear about informing Sally. Mary wanted to move into her house. Mary had no conflicting emotions when it came to the coldness and the darkness of her conscience.

Robert and his sister were very close, and he didn't want to hurt her. With Sally, material things had no value, and Sally's heart was pure and priceless. Mary forced him to tell Sally she wanted her house. The feeling Robert had to bear telling his sister what Mary wanted would leave an imprint in his heart for the rest of his life.

When Mary's mother died, everything on him had doubled. And what hurt him the most was how she would get angry at him for not being able to give her money to go shopping.

Still, she was his wife, and he had to tell his sister Sally that Mary wanted to move into her own house. He felt so small having to uproot his sister and giving her so short of a notice. At the time, he didn't realize Mary's motive was to get his sister out of their house.

Mary finally moved to Mississippi, taking Nora with her, putting him in more debt because of having to take care of two houses now instead of one.

Robert kept Mary informed on everything that went on since he was still in Peoria, taking care of her daughter Tammy. He received a check for a small amount from an attorney for a lawsuit in his and her name only because she was his wife. Since she wasn't there, she told him to sign her name on the check to cash it. Little did Robert know she was going to try to blackmail him for signing her name.

Robert remained in Peoria with Tammy. One day Mary's oldest daughter, Terry, asked him why her mother was in Mississippi and he was still here. It was as though it was his idea for Mary to leave her youngest daughter during her pregnancy, when she needed her mother the most.

He replied, "What your mother and I decide is none of your business." And he didn't care what she thought, but little did she know her mother made that decision and not him; and yet he was the one being blamed. After Mary had been staying in Mississippi for about six weeks, she told him she wanted to come back to Peoria.

Robert agreed and told her his daughter knew a schoolteacher who wanted to rent the house. She said she didn't want another woman in her house—that the house wasn't theirs anymore but hers. He was so frustrated with her for making things so hard until they turned into a nightmare.

He just threw his hand up and told her to put the house on the market, leaving his older daughter Tasha in the house until it was sold. Tasha was eighteen years old at the time. And Mary returned to Peoria. The schoolteacher who wanted to rent the house was a friend of the family's on Tasha's mother side and had always been a mother figure for Tasha. Robert never had a chance to meet her, but Tasha and her mother's family spoke highly of her.

His daughter called him and told him the schoolteacher had spent the night over because she had been on the highway a long time and was too tired to drive. Tasha called Mary to let her know as well.

Mary came to him in an outrage, saying, "You brought another woman into my house." She had caught him totally off guard. He didn't understand why she was angry. His daughter didn't have to be honest and tell them anything, and they never would have known, and yet she was accusing him of something he had no control of. He told her Tasha told him only after the fact.

Robert was very consistent with trying to settle things with Mary in order to ensure a peaceful divorce. He couldn't escape her nagging anymore because now his job was in a new location, and putting up with her nagging and wanting to fight wasn't his cup of tea.

She was a veteran at fighting from her previous marriage, trained and ready for battle. Robert asked her again for a divorce, and unexpectedly, she agreed, and the joy he felt inside was overwhelming. He didn't care what the divorce cost; he was going to put it on a credit card. It would put him deeper in debt, but being in debt didn't compare to being incarcerated with the princess of evil.

Just the thought of having his freedom again and getting from around her was like being released from prison. He had already talked to an attorney; all he had to do was make an appointment for them both to sign the papers. He reassured her that she could keep their marital assets. All he wanted was his divorce. He told her the date and time of their appointment with the attorney. She was totally agreeable.

When it was time for them to meet with the attorney, they left home together, laughing and talking. Upon their arrival at the attorney's office, the attorney wanted to meet with Robert first, and then with both of them together. Robert explained to the attorney what he was giving Mary. Then the attorney asked him to go and get Mary, to see if his terms were acceptable to her.

When he got back to the waiting area, she was nowhere to be found. She had left him in the attorney's office and driven off, not even worrying about how he was getting home. He had to catch a city bus home, where she was waiting and started yelling at him at once. "I can't believe you had the nerve to bring me to an attorney's office."

He had to laugh over the way she had left him there, making him look stupid and catching the bus home. He had actually started to feel sorry for her again, and he tried to do this in a different approach. He decided he was going to be patient.

He had a habit of putting all his paycheck stubs in a shoebox on top of the drawer, so she had knowledge of his weekly salary. One day he observed that all his paycheck stubs were missing. He instantly put two and two together and figured she had her own attorney and was preplanning this divorce.

Before she realized it, he knew what was going on. When she returned home, he gave her a chance to put his payroll check stub back in the box. He left the room, pretending he had to go to the restroom.

When he returned to the bedroom, all his paycheck stubs were back in the box. He asked her why she took them, and she replied sarcastically, "I went to see my own attorney, and he told me to tell you, if you don't give me what I want, you're going to jail for signing my name on the check you signed when I was in Mississippi."

He replied, "The check you told me to sign."

She nodded with a smile, saying, "I advised you to give me what I want."

She said she wanted him to sell the house and give her the money, and the rest of their marital assets, and her attorney told her to tell him to take out a loan to pay the car off and then put it in her name. And he was to pay her $1,000 a month in maintenance. Her overwhelming greed was trying to thread all of her greediness in the eye of a needle.

She tried to intimidate him by holding him hostage for a ransom of greed. It was as though she was saying, *You either live with me in my world, or live in your world with nothing.* In his mind, she was well beyond being an Indian giver, taking way more than what she gave. When she spoke, she spoke with authority, with confidence, as though she thought she was a prison guard threatening him with solitary confinement.

Robert chuckled. "You and your attorney can go to hell. If you think for any reason I'm going to let you take anything from me, you have another thing coming." From that point on, he knew he had to outsmart her and make her evil thoughts blast her in the face. He knew she thought she was going to take him to the bank, being that she was unemployed; and with her health condition, she knew she had the upper hand.

Again, Robert was filled with anger and wanted to beat her to a pulp. He went out and hired himself an attorney. He gave the attorney partial of his retainer fee; he would give him the rest when he served her the divorce papers.

But to be honest, Robert had to analyze the situation and look at his chances of winning from all angles; and the way things stood, he thought she would win, and also that she could stick him with a lifetime commitment, what with her being unemployed and sick.

He realized now why it was so hard for her to tell him what she wanted: she wanted all their assets and maintenance for the rest of her life. He had to turn his anger into a level tool to achieve victory over her in court. He didn't have to wonder; he knew he was going to have a very nasty divorce.

But in Robert's heart, he knew he would always have tried to be there for her. What he was so angry about was when she tried to blackmail him to get what she wanted. She was determined to win this at any cost, even if it meant taking away his freedom. With no doubt, he knew now that marrying her had been like entering the lion's den. Mary had now grown to be too sophisticated to settle for anything less than what she wanted. Robert's mind would drift, knowing he had to conquer his fear and control the things she thought he had no control of.

At this point, he knew he had to be an actor—kiss her when he should have been biting her, step over her when he should have been kicking her, and hug her when he should be pushing her away. He had to convince her he was in this marriage to stay and to gain her trust, letting her think she was in control. The cake he had baking for her had to have the right ingredients that were going to leave a bitter taste in her mouth, because no sugar was added.

Robert's mind drifted, and he wondered how he had ended up sleeping with the devil, eating with the devil, even going to church with the devil. Just thinking now of making love to her left no room to fantasize, but he had to gain her trust to defeat her in court. Even while making love to her, he stroked her with anger. But the harder he stroked, the more she wanted.

Mary's son heard about him wanting and pursuing a divorce, and it gave him courage to say what he had been holding back for years. Her son, who was in his early thirties, called the house; and when Robert picked up phone, he spoke with a sarcastic rudeness in his voice. "I heard you wanted to divorce my mother." And he went on to say he didn't like Robert anyway.

Robert never said a word; he just hung up the phone. He told her what her son had said, and she never replied. A couple of days later, she called him to stop by the house.

Upon her son's arrival, Robert asked him, did he have anything he wanted to say to him? Her son replied, "I am not like my sister. I will fuck you up." He tried to intimidate Robert by walking raggedly up to him with his mother standing in the middle. He pushed his mother to the side, but it didn't take him long to realize he had made a big mistake.

He got back in his car, but not without threatening Robert. "I'm going to get you."

Without hesitation, Robert called the police to file a report, and the next day, he filed a restraining order—only in case Mary's son tried to fulfill his threat. A few days later, Robert's baby daughter Nora overheard Mary having a conversation with her son, trying to get him to press charges against Robert.

Robert couldn't say anything to Mary about what his daughter had told him. He chuckled, not understanding how she could cut off the hand that was feeding her.

Even with her kids, he had always shown them love and had their best interest at heart. And he gave Mary his last, taking on his responsibility as a husband. He couldn't help but think back to her sickness. How he told her to let him know when she was about to run out of medication, because her medication came first, even if he had to charge it to his credit card—how he had always put her first.

The kindness she had shown him and his kids was only a cover to hide her hardheartedness and coldness, her focus on personal gain. And even her kind smile—her lips covered the teeth of a shark that was waiting to rip him apart. She had many people fooled with her kind ways and an upside-down smile of caring, but her heart was so far away.

He wanted a divorce so bad he could taste his freedom once and for all, but he still had her well-being in mind. He was so miserable; she was like a bad toothache giving him so much pain, and he would do anything for relief.

He had a mixture of hurt and anger bottle up within. He thought of his wife trying to get him locked up by trying to persuade her son to press charges against him.

And knowing her son was wrong to trespass in their marriage, especially when he had a history of domestic battery putting his hands on his own child's mother. And not once in Robert's marriage did he ever put his hands on his wife, but it was all right for Mary's son to put his hands on the mother of his child. What a hypocrite.

Robert's anger was taking him to another level, to the point of seeking another attorney. He was hoping to find the right combination that would get him free from the iron bars of his marriage, where there were no windows and no sign of daylight that seemed to be a conviction of solitary confinement for the rest of his life.

Filled with anger, he made up his mind to go ahead with the divorce. He went and hired another attorney, knowing that with Mary sick and unemployed, he was feeding himself to the sharks. This was like a lifetime commitment or taking the chance of some other man marrying her. Many attorneys would tell you they can do this or they can do that like they have your best interest at heart, until they get your money. Then afterward, they would tell you what they can do within the law is limited.

Once Robert got back home, he thought things over again. He decided to put his anger aside and be an actor, because he realized he had to fight for his life. In fact, it was a life sentence, with no parole. He just wanted her out of his life. And when he was reminded of how she treated him, he just refused to pay her restitution for her greed, which had been her intention from day one.

He called his attorney to inform him not to serve her any paper yet, that he would notify him when he wanted the papers to be served. The attorney asked him why, and he replied the timing was wrong. "I have to work on her income first." What puzzled him the most was that his attorney represented himself as God Almighty, knowing he was going to be butchered by the facts of his case and, according to the law, giving him no defense in the fight.

What stayed in Robert's mind was that everyone he talked to highlighted their thoughts of defeat and told him he had no way out of this but to give her what she wanted or hope the judge would award her less than what she was trying to get. What kept ringing in his head, the voice of many people, was that he would have to give her something.

Everyone thought he was silly to try to fight a battle that had already been won. First of all, he knew he had to overcome his fear of the seed of defeat that other people had planted in his mind. And the things he had to do, it wasn't in his nature to play the character he had to play. It was time to hit her below the belt, with no holds barred.

He had so many thoughts of things he had to do just stampeding in his mind, but everything had to be clockwork, and timing was the most important thing. He had to convince her that him wanting to divorce her was a thing of the past. And to be too anxious was like a bomb that could blow him right out of the water, which was why timing and patience were key. She had shielded herself by keeping her guard up. When she threw him salt, he accommodated her with sugar.

She later informed him that her doctor told her she had to have surgery, and him being there for her wasn't part of the act. Being there with her came from the heart, but it still convinced her that divorce was out of his system. Right after she got out of the hospital, he surprised her with a newer car, fully loaded. The corruption of his marriage was sugar-coated with kindness to materialize her thoughts of the hardship in their marriage of a divorce.

CHAPTER 10

The Strategy

I
T WAS LATER WHEN ROBERT'S baby daughter Nora started to speak
out about how Mary had physically abused her, leaving bruises and
welts all over her body by beating her with a belt and the heel of her
shoe. Nora was really terrified of Mary and afraid that if she spoke out,
something bad would happen to her.

When Robert approached her and asked her about beating his child
like that in a roundabout way, she replied that she had asked Nora to
clean her room, and that she was sniffling. He replied, "You mean you
beat my child like that because she was sniffling." He told her very firmly,
"If you put another mark on her again, you will pay the consequences,
even if it means I'm going to jail." It wasn't a threat but a promise.

His daughter also informed him this wasn't the first time Mary had abused her. She also said Mary had left bruises on her face, but then used cocoa butter to try to clear up her bruises. This happened while he was out of town.

After Robert heard this, he was even more determined not to give Mary the victory in court by paying her any maintenance. He hardened his heart for revenge, and just the thought of what his daughter had been through broke his heart because it was his responsibility to protect her. He felt so much anger he shook his head, saying to himself that he wasn't going to give her a cent.

His thoughts were not only on winning his divorce case. Deep down, being that cruel wasn't in his character. His only concern was getting out from under the muscle of marriage that she was using to crush him.

Her actions borne out of the darkness of her conscience against his kids gave him the strength to defeat her in court. He was now thinking, *Bitch, it's time to play.* His deepest thoughts were that it was sad when two people were joined as one but had to be divided for the other half to survive; but then again, it was no different when half of a person's body had to be amputated for the other half to live.

His first task was to try to generate some type of income for her without her getting suspicious of what he was trying to do. He introduced his concern to her by showing interest in her health. Because of her condition, she had been unemployed about ninety days and wouldn't be looking for a job because of it, which made her qualify for her social security benefits.

And he convinced her to apply. But in the same token, it could also prove that she was totally unable to work. If her social security was approved, he could be shooting himself in the foot. Then again, he felt it was better to shoot himself in the foot than to let her shoot him in the head being incarcerated and living in the pits of hell of their marriage with her for the rest of his life.

However, if her social security was approved, she would be covered under Medicare, and it would protect him from her attorney coming after him with the COBRA law. The spouse who is covered by the employee health care plan may choose to retain their group health coverage after a divorce or a legal separation from the employee. The judge could have him or her pay the health care coverage up to three years, which could be very expensive as an out-of-the-pocket expense.

Mary was full of greed, and getting her social security was well overdue. He went to the Social Security office with her to apply. Having such greed, she even falsified her marital status as married but separated to get her full disability benefits. She said that she knew what she was doing, and also that she was using her ex-husband's last name instead of her present married name.

The woman claimed to be a saint but had the mind of a criminal. She also denied applying for her unemployment benefit after the death of her mother and denied to the social security officer that she had applied for her unemployment benefit as well. As the old saying goes, "Never throw a brick when you are living in a glass house yourself."

And being the first to criticize others for their action, yes, she was a hypocrite who hid her greed behind the church doors and camouflaged with her smile the coldness of her heart.

After weeks had passed, Mary waited for Social Security to make a decision. She was denied, so Robert told her to file an appeal with the Social Security office.

After another long wait, the Social Security office wanted Mary to be examined by another physician. After setting her appointment, and after being examined by the Social Security physician, she was denied again for benefits. Again, Robert told her to file an appeal with the Social Security office for them to reverse their decision.

After weeks had passed, the Social Security office made arrangements for a court hearing, and Robert knew it was time to do his homework. He instructed Mary to get her medical records and have her doctor write up a statement explaining why she was unable to work, and all of this had to be done before her court appearance.

Upon her court appearance, after the review of her medical file and fighting for her benefit for over a year, Mary's social security was finally approved.

After a year, Robert's attorney called him to see if he was ready to serve her with the divorce papers. He informed his attorney he still wasn't ready yet.

Robert's next move was to still generate her more income by convincing her to start her own business. He asked her how she would like to have her own cleaning business. Once again, she was overjoyed in her greed, and was very excited about having her own business. And she was really excited over beating the system Immediately, he made her flyers and some business cards to advertise her business.

About a week later, she got her first customer. She was so happy she was drowning in tears. He told her that since she didn't have a checking account, he would open her one in his name and add her name to the account. Which meant he would have access to all of her clients' canceled checks that her clients wrote her for proof of her employment and her ability to work and taking care of herself. About a week later, another person called for her services. Slowly but surely, one client after another was calling her.

Robert spoke with his attorney again, informing him she was on social security and had started her own business, but that he needed more time for her business to generate more clients. And she was so good with her business that she got many of her clients through word of mouth. He also convinced her that since she was expanding, she needed to keep records of her earnings, and the names and addresses and phone numbers of all her clients.

He bought her a record notebook to do so. He noticed that when she finished recording her clients and her earnings, she would hide her book.

Having gone through the torment he did with Mary in the past, Robert trained himself to have patience—nothing but patience, even if it meant lifting every piece of furniture and turning back every rug, looking behind every dresser and going through every drawer and looking in every crack that was large enough for her to hide her record book.

One day, while she was at work, he searched the house and found her recording book on the floor in the living room underneath the coffee table. The book contained the names of all her clients. Her business was really picking up. He made copies of her record book and put it back the exact way he had found it, to keep her from suspecting what he was doing.

As Mary's business continued to grow, he increased her hourly rate two dollars more for all new customers. Besides, her income was really starting to grow. He would wait for a few weeks before he would attempt to copy her client book again.

Her recorder book would never be in the same place. She kept putting it in difference locations. It wasn't that she was hiding her record book because she had caught on to what he was doing. She was hiding it for her sense of greed; she didn't want anyone to know how much her income was. It was like he had a built-in GPS system, finding it to update his files. He took nothing for granted, He had set up something he called the scan-and-put-back rule. When she received her Medicare card, he scanned it into his computer and then put it back.

Mary was so good at what she did, and she was very well liked by one of her clients, who wrote an article in the newspaper about her in reference to her business. She was so proud of herself, and so was Robert. He found the article and scanned it and then put it back. The article also proved her business did exist. He also found the letter of approval from Social Security, and he scanned it too.

In his search for her record book, he found many things in reference to her—her school records and her birth certificate. He took nothing for granted; he scanned them and then put them back.

She also had some outstanding debts, but the ones that were the most outstanding were her medical bills, which were up for collection. He knew that in the state where they lived, her debts were his debts, and his debts were her debts. He knew he had to eliminate all her debts, especially her doctor's bills; otherwise the judge could make him pay all her debts or award her maintenance to help pay off her debts.

The only way he could do this was to file for bankruptcy, something he hated to do because of his credit. He convinced her that since her credit was bad anyway, it was better for both of them to file for bankruptcy. And both of them had to do it together to be protected under the bankruptcy law. He managed to eliminate all her debts, and right after, he received their discharge papers.

He managed to slowly but surely start his credit over by putting a thousand dollars in a CD account.

And he borrowed a thousand against his CD account, generating some credit for himself, which helped him to generate more credit elsewhere, to show the court he was the one in debt. But he was willing to negotiate with her under the state law. His debts were her debts, and her debts were his debts, because she was his wife at the time. He eliminated her debts and raised his own.

On the other hand, because she was his wife, all the utilities were still in her name before they got married. He also had complete access to all her utility bills to be able to pay them each month. He had set up all her utility bills online so that he would be able to keep track of them while going through the divorce. He knew she was a liar, and besides, until the divorce was finalized, he wanted so much to be by her side, in case her sickness ever got worse; but in the back of his mind, he still thought of how she had abused his kids and tried to destroy him.

He also knew he had to sell their home before the attorney served her the divorce papers because their home being in the picture could prolong the divorce proceeding even more. And he could have more control of the equity they had in the home. After the home was sold, he tricked her by using the equity to pay off the very first car he had bought her, since that was in his name.

Then a few weeks later, he traded off her car and got himself a 2003 X5 BMW. The equity in their home was a little over $7,000, and the BMW dealership allowed him over the amount of the equity they got back from the house he had sold. Which meant he got all the equity on their home without giving her a cent.

Needless to say, Robert worked all the time. He did not want to park his X5 on the employee parking lot because dings other employees had experienced. He let her drive his X5, and he drove her other vehicle to work, which was a bad decision on his part since she was getting very attached to his vehicle.

She would always comment on how she loved the BMW X5. He started to realize his BMW wouldn't be in his best interest in the eyes of the judge. He felt the judge would think that if he could afford to drive a BMW, he could afford to give her maintenance money. After giving the matter a thoughtful consideration, he got off one evening without telling her anything and traded his BMW off for a Chevrolet Monte Carlo.

He arrived home late that evening, not saying one word of having a new car in the garage. The next morning, he stayed in the same routine of driving her vehicle and letting her drive his. He got a call early that morning from her, asking him what was the Monte Carlo was doing in the garage. He replied, "You'll like it." He could imagine what was going through her mind: *This man has lost his mind.* Instead, all she just said was "Oh."

Also, he observed her getting attached to the Monte Carlo, so he traded it in for a Chevrolet Silverado, and he ended up selling it to his cousin for an earlier-model truck. Making all these transactions he did with the trade-in of all these vehicles had eaten up all the money he had received from the equity of their home. And yet even that was fine. He was still able to throw a wrench in her greedy pursuit of the equity on their home for herself, threatening to blackmail him by incarceration.

Robert began to trust his instincts amid all the commotion of keeping her from taking her frustration out on his baby daughter. It was better to get her out of harm's way, so he took Nora to stay with her sister for the entire school year, and until he was able to gather all the evidence he needed to defeat Mary in court.

He knew his daughter staying with his sister was only a temporary move because he needed her for a shield, to show the court he was still supporting his daughter, which would play a major factor. He knew no judge would take from a child to give to a person who was working and able to work, when he had proven she was getting enough income to take care of herself.

When the day came for him to make his move, he knew she was capable of paying for all her living expenses, without getting any support from him. Robert would not be giving her any money whatsoever to help her to pay for anything. She could use it in court to show him giving her support for her to survive. He had to prove she was able to stand on her own without his support and that her living condition never changed after he had left her.

Besides his full-time job, Robert had started his own lawn care business, and he knew he had to prove his lawn care business no longer existed. He placed an ad in the newspaper three months before leaving her: "Lawn care equipment for sale, going out of business, must sell." He knew he could use the newspaper ad as a legal document to show in court that his lawn care business no longer existed. And he wrote a letter to all his clients saying that for medical reasons, he would be unable to maintain their yard.

Before placing the ad, he had given her brother a job with him doing lawn care. And after months had passed and he no longer needed her brother's services, he could have him subpoenaed to testify as to the last time he worked for him in his lawn care business. In fact, her brother's wife could be subpoenaed as well.

Having her brother and her sister-in-law subpoenaed would work in his favor. Her brother could testify he no longer worked for Robert, whose business no longer existed.

He would attempt to protect his retirement by proving she had her own business and by him giving her the marital asset that they had agreed on, which had more value at the time than he had in his retirement. The judge could only award her from the time of their marriage and from the time of their divorce. She would get only what she would be entitled to. Robert was so deep into his planning. It would be beyond her imagination, and would leave her no room for any negotiations.

CHAPTER 11

A Stranger He Never Knew

MARY WAS WELL KNOWN AND well liked in the little town where she lived. Her counterfeit ways of being so meek and humble was very convincing and made it easy for her to persuade others into seeing things her way. She appeared to be an angel sent from heaven. When she spoke, she spoke with so much concern and caring, but behind closed doors, her image of trust left a reflection of the Antichrist. She was a wolf in sheep's clothing, her cosmetic appearance hiding the true image of the ugliness that dwelt within.

She scalded and branded Robert with her words, ridiculing and disgracing his name. He could see the attention in other people's eyes as they stared at him. They saw him as the wolf that blew their house down. But Robert had to ask himself, *How can a wolf blow down a strong and solid foundation of a relationship that was never built? And how can you made a withdrawal when nothing was deposited?*

He was convicted without a chance to put up his defense, but only by her words; and the abuse she put his kids through obviously had no value. If they were God, he would have been dead, and his soul would be tormented in hell for eternity.

It didn't take long for Robert to realize that Mary was getting worse. Her recklessness and rudeness stood firm in showing him the woman he had really married. Surely, she wasn't an angel disguised as a saint with the heart of a beast. She repeatedly told him how she wanted to have a gun to shoot him, and she would say, "I am not going to kill you. I'll just shoot you in the leg."

One time, they were out for a ride, and she brought him to a gun store to fill out a gun permit. He watched her quietly out of the corner of his eyes, and she had a devilish look in her eyes when she glanced at him. He looked away as his mind drifted. He chuckled, saying to himself, *This bitch is crazy.* There wasn't any time for him to stick around to find out if she was a great shot. But one thing was for sure: he knew that he was allergic to knives and guns. He knew his time with her was coming to an end; it was time for him to turn the page.

She was still like a demon in the bedroom—totally insane, shattering glass against the wall, the sound echoing all throughout the house. Her footsteps sounded like those of a giant's, thudding like a drum, and he could see her with blood running down her arm, dripping to the floor. Her eyes would just flicker, and he was waiting for her neck to twist around on her shoulders, waiting to see if she was going to crawl on the ceiling and scratch out his toenail. Seriously, he did not know what to expect next and what she was capable of doing.

All kinds of objects flying around him in the bedroom, and never once did he look up. He just finished what he was doing, and afterward, showing no pity, he said, "You need to find a bandage and clean up this mess."

But she didn't stop there. She had filled people's minds with rumors, telling them how she left her own pregnant daughter in Peoria to go to Mississippi to take care of his kids. Telling them he had so many women; she even told them about the schoolteacher his daughter had let stay in the house. She was like a wild boar, ready to attack anyone and anything that stood in her way. She once took a hammer and smashed his cell phone in so many pieces. He named her the Queen of Drama.

During the time his daughter Nora was away at his sister's, Robert took Mary to his job's Christmas party. She was very happy and smiling the entire time. He thought they really had a good time together. But upon their return home, she went straight to his closet and started pulling out his clothes, telling him to get out. She caught him totally off guard because of her easygoing behavior earlier in the evening. Afterward, she picked up the phone and called the police, as though he was a threat to her. When the police arrived, she was all arrogance and outrage.

He never said one word to her. The police asked him, would he mind leaving just for the meantime? One of the officers came to him and told him he could see the problem was with her and not him. The officer said her behavior was uncalled for—the way she was acting with, all the yelling. "You never said one word."

Robert felt his silence would let her reveal her true image. He stayed at a hotel for a couple of nights. Then out of nowhere, she called and asked him when he was coming back home. "I didn't mean for you to not come back home."

He was saying in the back of his mind, *This bitch is really crazy. The bitch has a serious case of Alzheimer's, forgetting all that she had done, or she was playing a very stupid role, or thinking I'm as stupid as she is.* Her attitude gave him more of a 3D vision to look deeper within her to know what kind of person he was dealing with—someone who was just out to destroy him.

Still, he knew that being on the outside looking in would make it much harder for him to finish putting all of his evidence together, leaving him no choice but to keep telling himself he would be able to defeat her in court.

After her brother heard what happened, he told Robert, "She is trying to get you locked up and make you lose your job." No doubt, she didn't have his best interest at heart. At night, while he slept, she would prowl through the darkness in their driveway, searching through his truck to find any trace of another woman's belongings. Even at night, her mind would never rest.

She took money out of his ashtray and destroyed his checkbooks, as though someone else had been in his truck. At one time, he even accused her brother, who was living with them at the time, of going in his truck. Later, after he had investigated the matter, he found out she was the one who had been in his truck and was willing to make her brother take the blame.

The more contact he had with his family and friends, the worse she exercised her rudeness by hanging up the phone while he was talking. His sister and cousins would always tell Robert to give her the phone so she could verify who he was talking to. He refused to do so, because his conversation with them spoke for itself. He felt that the way a person carried themselves always spoke for itself, and no words needed to be spoken. It got to a point where many of his family members wouldn't call because of the confusion involved in calling his household.

After the school year, he brought his daughter Nora back to Peoria. She really didn't want to go back, but she missed her family, especially her big sister Tasha, whom she looked up to. Still, it was not easy for her to return to the house of horror, where she was abused. A short time later, her sister Tasha returned to Peoria, pregnant.

Robert was very happy to have both of his daughters back in the same house, and Nora could feel less threatened than she did being with Mary alone. Every day when he entered the house after work, they would gather in his bedroom, overjoyed to be in his presence. Again, Mary would accuse them of stopping their conversation when she entered the room, as though to say he and his daughters were talking about her. Her destructive mind would never sleep.

She was actually jealous of his close relationship with his daughters, not only with the two in Peoria but also with his daughter in New Orleans. Little did he know that in her mind, she wasn't looking at them as his daughters but as other women. In fact, in her eyes, all the female members of his family were other women.

He was a bus driver, and one of his supervisors advised him that he had observed his wife following his bus in her car at night, and thought it was very weird. Robert had no idea she had gotten to the point of stalking him.

Nora was out of school for the summer, but in a week or so, school would be starting again, and he had very little time to get her school clothing together.

Tasha called him and told him Kmart had a big sale on back-to-school clothing. He called Mary to tell her that he was going to Kmart when he got off from work to pick up some school clothes for Nora, and did she want to come along? But she didn't answer her phone.

After Robert got off from work, he picked up his two daughters to go to Kmart. Mary was nowhere to be found. About fifteen minutes after they had arrived at Kmart, Mary called Tasha's cell phone and asked her where they were. Tasha passed the phone to Robert, saying, "Daddy, it's Mary."

He took his daughter's phone to tell Mary they were in Kmart. She replied, "Yes, I know. I am down the aisle looking at you." He looked down the aisle and saw her staring at him as she walked toward him down the aisle.

The look in her eyes was as though she had caught him with two women instead of his daughters. In fact, he still didn't think she was jealous of his own daughters and was looking at them as potential lovers. Her jealousy had started to show, but never in a million years did he think she was that disorientated to the point of being overtaken by jealousy.

When he and the kids returned home, her ridiculous attitude was an outrage. His older daughter heard them quarreling over him taking Nora shopping for school clothes. Tasha was disturbed to hear them arguing, and getting even louder. Tasha tried to keep the peace: "Daddy, don't worry about it."

Mary stood up and faced her. "What do you mean 'don't worry about it'?" She raised her hand slapping Tasha, trying to provoke her.

But Tasha still respected her, so she just walked away. Robert felt like grabbing Mary around the neck and choking her without mercy, but he knew she was trying to provoke him to hit her. Instead, he said to her, "You have no right to lay your hand on my daughter."

He went to Tasha's bedroom to see if she was all right, and Mary came in and slapped Tasha again. This time Tasha reached out, grabbed Mary, wrestled her to the floor, and landed on top of her. And Robert did nothing to stop his daughter. He just stood there and let his daughter beat his wife's ass. At the moment, he really wanted his daughter to get her revenge on Mary for slapping her and give Mary the ass beating he wanted to give her. But being a man, he stood still. His action spoke for itself: he was getting tired of Mary's behavior.

Tasha eventually got off from on top of Mary, who had bitten her on the breast, leaving her teeth marks. When Robert saw the marks on his daughter's breast, he could have beaten Mary down without mercy. Even if he had gone insane beating her, it still wouldn't have undone what she had done to his daughter. Mary's reaction was like that of a mad dog that needed to be put on a leash.

Robert could have beaten her to death with his bare hands in front of his kids, but it would have marked them for life. For a moment, his mind drifted, and he heard Tasha's voice in the back of his mind saying to him one day, "Daddy, I hope nothing ever happens to you." It was as though she was saying, *You're all we got.* Hearing those words in his mind penetrated his heart. From that day on, his daughter had left an image of a broken mirror with no reflection, of a conscience that reflected no pity.

With tears in his eyes, he resolved even more to beat her in court. And what was more devastating was that after the divorce, his plan was to turn all his evidence over to Social Security so they could charge her with social security fraud. She was going down one way or another.

Mary went right away to her phone to call her baby daughter to come and jump on Tasha, after she realized Tasha was too much for her to handle. What was even more devastating was that Tasha had just had her baby and was still trying to recover. That same night, Mary's brother took Tasha and her baby to stay at his house after he found out about the confrontation between Mary and Tasha.

At this point, Robert knew it was time to let the attorney serve her the divorce papers. He really had to keep a level head and refrain from putting his hands on her, which would have made him the perpetrator. His mind filled with so many thoughts, including wanting to beat her ass; but instead, he focused on the incentive from doing his fighting in court, turning all his paperwork over to Social Security to bring her up on charges of fraud.

Shortly after his daughter had left Peoria, he once again asked Mary what she wanted if they decided to file for a divorce. He informed her that even after all he had been through, he would still give her all that was left of their marital assets, such as all their furniture, which were very expensive pieces, and that he would continue paying her car insurance until she had paid the car off.

She agreed to his offer, and he was at ease, thinking she was going to sign their divorce papers without a fight. He had already rented him an apartment and was furnishing it little by little. He did this right after her confrontation with Tasha, because he knew there was no way he could stay with her after she had bitten Tasha in the breast. Obviously, her actions spoke for itself. The years of their marriage had bought her time to take what she wanted, using his kids for security was obsolete.

Shortly after that, she stole and hid his phone and his checkbooks out of his truck and refused to give them back to him. She finally gave him his phone and told him she had thrown his checkbooks in a Dumpster. Robert, however, didn't believe she had done what she said she had done.

He just stopped asking her about his checkbooks, hoping she would give them back to him. Instead, she went on a warpath and threw everything in her sight against the wall and to the floor. The bedroom looked as though a tornado had been through it and left no signs of survivors. He was so angry with her he called her a bitch out loud.

She went to the kitchen and got a knife and started violently attacking him, swinging the knife at him in all directions. She managed to cut the tip of his finger when he took a clothes hanger and caught her wrist, snatching the knife out of her hand.

Nora ran in and retrieved the knife from the floor and took it to her bedroom. Mary went back to the kitchen and got another knife, saying, "Call me a bitch again." Right then and there, Robert forgot about her being a woman and told her, "Bitch, if you come at me again with that knife . . ." He held a lamp in his hand as she stood in the doorway. He would knock her out with the lamp in self-defense. His mind was made up this time to hurt her with no pity.

She got on the phone and called the police, and upon their arrival, she told the officers he had jumped on her and had hit her in the side of her face, causing it to swell. Her face was swollen because of the change in the weather that aggravated her sickness. He explained her sickness to the police, showing them the blood on his finger from when she had cut him.

She told the police she did it because he had called her a bitch. The police officer asked him, did he call her a bitch, and he denied it, because the word *bitch* didn't put her in harm's way and didn't mean he threatened her with bodily harm. The officer informed Mary she was going to jail.

The police had no other choice but to bring her to jail because blood had been spilled. Mary's attitude changed so quickly then: she ran to the bedroom crying and yelling, "Honey, please don't let them take me to jail." After her outrage and her rudeness, now she was crying like a baby, expecting him to be her pacifier. Little did she know he didn't have any say-so in the matter. It was too much of a liability issue for them not to take her to jail.

He chuckled, feeling no sympathy for her at all. Her uncalled-for behavior made him think of a wild female dog, untamed and far from being house-broken. A bitch that needed to be put in a cage.

She was taken out of the house screaming and hollering. Instead, he wanted to say, out of anger, "Put the bitch in the paddy wagon before she disturbs the neighbors." Having a hardened heart wasn't in Robert's character, but at the moment, he was just simply angry.

Robert, a man of character, wouldn't want to see a dog go to jail. Just her luck, unfortunately, that she wasn't a dog. He couldn't help looking the other way. It's true—it's a thin line between love and hate. A person who loved you once can hate you just as much. Mary's plans of getting Robert incarcerated had backfired from a door she had opened for him. The bed she had made for him was the bed she had to lie in. And it was only the beginning. He now had all the ammunition he needed to fight her in court.

The next day, Mary's daughter dropped her off at home, and Robert could feel the tension in the air, and the way her daughter stared at him as she pulled into the driveway. Mary entered the house and walked so softy throughout that you could hear a pin drop. She was so meek and humble; Robert wished she had stayed another day before Satan marked her territory, before he could make his move to get out.

He had hidden some of her belongings in exchange for his checkbooks. The next day, her brother told him that while he was at work, she called the police again to tell them he had stolen something from her and wanted him arrested. The police informed her that he was her husband and had the right to take whatever he wanted in the house. She didn't tell them she had stolen his checkbooks and was refusing to give them back. Her malicious ways and her stupidity filled him with bitterness. It was time to destroy her by exacting revenge in the courtroom.

It was time to serve her the divorce papers.

One Sunday morning, Mary got up to get ready for church. This very morning, he knew within himself that it was time for him to leave. As soon as he saw her pull out of the driveway, he took only his clothes and his daughters' bedroom set, leaving her with all the things they had verbally agreed on she could keep.

He left her a letter:

> You called the police on me for the last time. Why didn't you tell them you stole my checkbooks? Is this what this was about?

He felt as though he had just been released from prison, and now he could do whatever he wanted to keep from being in her trap again. He felt as though the whole world had just been lifted off his shoulders.

He didn't move into the first apartment he had rented; instead, he asked the apartment manager if he could break his lease, lying about how he had decided to stay with his wife, that he was not divorcing her. He figured it was a good reason, and the apartment manager would think he had reconciled with his wife. He lost his deposit, but the manager allowed him to break the lease.

He wanted to move far enough away that no one would know his whereabouts, and at a distance no one wanted to drive.

CHAPTER 12

Firing The Second Attorney and Hiring The Third

A FTER ROBERT HAD MOVED, HE called his attorney, anxious to get her behind him, to serve Mary her papers. He had paid his attorney $1,500 for his retainer fee and for his divorce papers to be filed in court. Mary called him to ask him to come back home, but the thought of all the hardships he and his daughters had gone through made coming back simply out of the question. She was now just a thing from the past. He knew it was time to let the chips fall wherever they may.

And more so with the ways she had abused his kids. She told her brother to tell Robert that he had mail at the house, and that he could pass by to pick it up. So Robert went to her house for his mail, and then she just starting crying, hoping he would have enough sympathy for her to come back home. She cried out loud, "I don't want a divorce."

He thought, *You may not want a divorce, but you are getting one.* She told him she had a big secret. "I have some money, and I want us to buy another house."

Robert just ignored what she said. All the money in the world wouldn't remove the bitterness she had put him and his kids through. Still, he couldn't help but wonder if her sisters were right when they accused her of taking out more insurance on their mother. She was so greedy that he wouldn't put it past her.

Still, he was willing to put the past behind him. And he would still be her friend. He did not know at the time that she had hired an attorney. She was seeking maintenance and his retirement and wanted him to pay her attorney's fees, and still wanted to keep the things he had left behind, as they had agreed.

Robert called his attorney to make an appointment. But on getting to his attorney's office, he met him in the hallway, and he told him he had to leave, but that he had spoken to Mary's attorney, with whom he was good friends. He told Robert about how Mary's attorney didn't want to hurt him, but only to get the things Mary was entitled to. Robert didn't get a chance to show his attorney he had prepared his whole case, that he only needed him as a mouthpiece and to take care of the legal aspects of his case. Because Robert knew that today's society was filled with politics.

After his attorney had said that he was good friends with Mary's attorney, Robert knew this attorney wouldn't have his best interest at heart. He didn't say a word; he just got back in the elevator and went to a different floor and hired another attorney fifteen minutes after his conversation with his attorney in the hallway.

Robert's new attorney informed him she had to get his file from his old attorney. After he finished telling her about his marriage, and about what he was up against, the first thing that came out of her mouth was, "You will have to give her something." He replayed the attorney's words and said, "No, I am not. I don't want to give her one penny."

He gave her a binder approximately an inch thick, which he had prepared himself. After she looked over the case Robert had prepared, she looked at him with delight and said, "Who put this together?"

Robert replied, "I did."

"You did a damn good job," she told him. But still, she wasn't the judge. But Robert knew he had to mastermind his own divorce, because attorneys only went by the law and the evidence that was put before them—not he-says or she-says evidence.

Robert's thoughts had no room for criticism, so he distanced himself from people who doubted him and believed he was fighting a losing battle. His wife slandered his name with everyone she knew and told many misleading stories of why he had left her, as though she was putting herself on trial in the streets, painting a picture of a perfect wife and a cheating husband. While she was trying to prove herself to other people, Robert was putting together more evidence to prove himself in court.

She bragged to other people, being very sarcastic and smiling an ironic smile, talking about how he cheated and now he was going to pay. She had no doubt at all about winning this divorce case. It was as though she had x-ray vision, but not knowing there was much more to life than met the human eye. She had counted her money before the judge had made his decision. Even her sister-in-law came to Robert and told him about how Mary was going around bragging about how she was going to make him pay her.

Robert could picture the scenario in his mind, and the words of her sister-in-law kept ringing in his ears: *He's going to pay me.* He could also picture how she had abused his kids, and how he had to put up with all of her nagging and the domestic violence that she had put him through, and he vowed that paying her for her abuse was out of the question. He would always be haunted by how he had misjudged her and how his kids had ended up being the victims, and how the experience would stay in his kids' minds for the rest of their lives.

Robert thought about her devilish ways, how she slapped him in the face too many times, and how she wanted to gain victory over him in court, making him pay her maintenance, as though he was applauding her for her abuse and her greed. Even the thought of paying her for a lifetime would only reveal the hardship that would linger in the shadows of his mind for the rest of his life.

His anger toward her was so deep-seated, but he refused to be overthrown by anger in the streets, knowing his battlefield was the courthouse. And her transgressions against his kids left no room for restitution for her; instead, she had to suffer the consequences. His anger was not going to be physically manifested; he was just going to beat her legally, in the presence of the judge, and he would show no mercy.

CHAPTER 13

The Other Woman

ABOUT SEVEN MONTHS LATER, ROBERT met a girl named Gail. She had just gotten hired where he was employed. She seemed familiar, like he had seen her before but he couldn't remember where. One day, being serious minded, he asked her, had they met before? She said she didn't think so. But still, he really thought he had seen her before.

Gail was an easygoing person, and a spiritual type. In fact, she was also Pentecostal, the same as Robert's two previous wives. As time went by, he loved to tease her by sneaking up behind her, scaring her. She had no idea he had been married or that he was going through a divorce.

Every day he found himself teasing her more and more, although he viewed her only as a coworker and a good friend. Neither of them viewed each other as being more than just a friend.

Gail had a great sense of humor and a soft smile. Her spirit resurrected his in his depressing moments brought on by the divorce. Being in her company interrupted his crowded thoughts of the hardship he was going through with Mary. Nevertheless, his thoughts of his wife were like a bad infection that had spread all over his body. He was angry with her for biting his daughter—a nightmare that just wouldn't go away.

Many days, his mind would drift, and he would think about how he should have just strangled Mary with his bare hands after she had bitten Tasha. And when his mind backtracked on how Mary abused his daughters, the hate that he felt lingered in his mind, strengthening his determination to defeat her in court. Gail helped him in many ways to ignore his feelings about Mary, feelings that had waxed cold.

As his friendship with Gail grew, he eventually told her about his marriage and his divorce.

She asked him, "Is she saved in a spiritual way?"

He told her about how Mary had disgraced his name, making him look like the bad guy with all her false accusations.

Overlooking Mary's stupidity, Robert knew he still had to stay focused and channel his anger through the court justice system; but the more he talked about Mary, the angrier he felt. She was like a throbbing pain in his side, and he didn't see any relief.

He started teasing Gail more each day, saying, "You're going to be my next wife. You are my baby." She would just smile, not saying anything, as though to say, *Yeah, right.* In fact, he was just teasing her, not knowing his teasing was going to lead into a relationship. And she was going to be caught up in the crossfire of his divorce. An innocent victim who would be caught up in a drive-by. Mary would destroy her by ridiculing her and anyone else who stood in her way.

Robert was so much older than Gail—in fact, eighteen years older—and he viewed her more as a daughter than a lover. But he loved being in her company. Unconsciously, he was beginning to develop feelings for her. And she was the only person who was willing to listen to what he was going through in his marriage and divorce. Still, she stayed neutral, but willing to listen, without criticizing him like everyone else did. Mary had poisoned people's minds with overrated stories of Robert being a bad guy.

Gail was such an inspiration to Robert, calming down his doubts about everyone looking down on him, thanks to the false accusations that Mary had spread abroad.

The very first time he realized he was falling for her was when he sneaked behind her to scare her and she had said, "Robert, please stop scaring me." He looked at her with passion and replied, "I will." And she said, "You promise?" He replied, "Yes, I promise." Still, he would tease her by telling her she was going to his wife and his baby. And she would just smile.

But he started to believe the words he spoke. Their conversations would only be at work in person or over the phone while at work, but never at home or when they weren't working—until one day when she called him and asked him what he was doing, in a roundabout way. From that point on, their friendship had begun to turn in a different direction.

He visited her church, and she looked a lot different there out of her work uniform. She was stylishly dressed, and the smell of her perfume influenced his attraction toward her. He was sold by the words that came out of her mouth. She would say the man who found her found a good thing, and she would always be obedient to her husband.

Her words influenced his deep thoughts about her, and she was influenced by his words, by him saying, "You're going to be my wife." Both of them were overthrown by the words out of their mouth, and found themselves eager to get married after his divorce.

Gail had said some words that were wedged in his mind. She said she had always wanted to marry a preacher.

And she said she had asked God for someone who had more than she had, or was her equal. In Robert's mind, it didn't matter what a person had in the material world; what mattered was that he was willing to share the little bit he did have. What was more important to him was what was in the heart. In his mind, no woman could be as bad as the one he was trying to divorce. He and Gail even went so far as to try to plan for their wedding.

But Robert knew everything about his relationship with Gail had to be confidential. He didn't want anyone to know; he didn't need any obstacle in his way to divorcing Mary. But Gail was excited, and eventually slipped, telling many people of her impending marriage, which badly hurt Robert's chances in court.

He was working late one night, and while at work, he could see Gail's house from a distance. He saw a car in her driveway; it was the same color as Mary's, but he thought it couldn't be his wife's car. Later, when he called Gail, he could tell by her voice that something was wrong. With no hesitation, he asked, "Did Mary come by your house?"

She hesitated for a moment and then replied, "Yes, but she told me not to tell you she came by my house."

Gail was labeled as a home wrecker, the woman who broke up Robert's marriage. Both Mary and Gail were with the Pentecostal Church of God and Christ. Mary went to Gail's pastor and everyone she knew, beguiling them, scandalizing Robert's and Gail's names, talking about how Gail was having an affair with her husband.

Gail was an innocent victim caught in the line of fire, hurt by the words out of Mary's mouth, which was throwing more gasoline into the fire. Gail's pastor came to Robert to tell him about what his wife had said about his affair with Gail. Even with Gail's pastor, Mary had labeled Gail as a home wrecker.

Needless to say, Gail had no idea why she had become Mary's target. It seemed as though everyone in their little town knew about the affair, but no one knew Robert didn't even know Gail when he was still married. The picture Mary had painted of Gail was the picture everyone viewed her as. Mary did everything she knew to destroy Robert and Gail. And with many people, Mary's word was gold. Mary was the most evil-minded person Robert had met, but she had already influenced many people's perceptions.

With Mary's words, many thought Gail and Robert had gotten married before Robert had divorced Mary. Gail, however, continued boldly talking about her affair with Robert, not knowing the hardship she was causing. Mary even went by Gail's house again, falsely accusing him about all the women Robert had supposedly had affairs with.

Robert didn't want to hurt Gail's feelings, but he wished she would keep her mouth shut until his divorce was final. Instead, her talking just added more stress to the situation. And her gossip was topped off with the subpoena that arrived after his attorney had told him so.

Robert told Gail she was going to be served a subpoena, but Gail was able to escape the subpoena, not being at home when it was served. Mary wanted Gail to testify about their affair and of Robert's intent to marry her or about being married to Robert before their divorce. She was attempting to use Gail as a tool to fight him in court.

Not only was Robert exhausted with his divorce, but his affair with Gail was also beginning to become a big turnoff for other people, who now knew too much of their business. Gail's motives were pure and innocent; she was filled with the excitement of being married, but Mary used her motives as dirt to disgrace her and Robert. What was so amazing about Gail was that nothing Mary did or said to influence her made her have a change of heart.

Gail's mother was very supportive. She didn't judge Robert by the rumors Mary had spread; she judged him according to his character. In Robert's subconscious mind, he distanced himself from many people whose minds he felt Mary had poisoned. He knew Mary had no intention to stop with her accusations, but she, however, underestimated Robert's drive to defeat her just because he was silent.

However, Robert didn't give a damn what people thought of him, refusing to let anyone dictate his life, because they weren't the ones who had to live with Mary in a world she thought revolved around her. At times, while he was at work, Mary would stop by to talk to him, with this *I got you* glance, saying in a calm manner, "Where have you been? I miss you." It was as though she was giving him an invitation to her bedroom, but she would never mention Gail; in fact, she would act as though Gail didn't even exist.

As Robert looked in her devilish eyes, sitting quietly in the driver's seat, he would think to himself, *This woman has to be intoxicated.* He was totally stunned by her freakish come-on. Clearing his throat, he would say to her, "It's time for me to go." And he would leave her, like she was the wind at his back.

Even at times when Mary would come knocking at his apartment, he wouldn't let her in. She knew he was serious and wasn't going to let her get in his bed, and he didn't want to get in her bed either.

With all her abuse of him and his kids and all her false accusations against him, he wanted her to pay the consequences—not in her bed but in court, where he would defeat her and shatter her sense of greed.

During this time, the daughter of Robert's sister Sally had died. Mary had known his niece very well during the course of her marriage to Robert. Grieving over his niece, he decided to tell Mary's brother to tell her Lisa had died. Lisa treated Mary with high respect. Mary's brother came back and told Robert that Mary had asked, "What are you telling me for?"

Her reaction was exactly like that of the beast she was. Robert wondered how anyone could hate so much and have a heart of stone. Mary's heart had waxed cold, no passion at all. How much hate could one endure?

Gail had never met Lisa, but she had shown more sympathy for a person she had never met, when Mary had sat down with Lisa at the same table and eaten of the same bread. Her hate was so deep she even cursed the grounds Robert's family walked on. Robert knew that with God, he could endure all things. Mary continued campaigning in the streets, filling it with gossip, spreading rumors door to door, church by church, and corner by corner, with anyone who would listen. And her next step would be the courtroom.

No marriage license was bought and no wedding ceremony was performed because of the words coming out of Mary's mouth. Gail and Robert were married behind closed doors. Mary was acting on her hate, being too dumb to realize the words she was looking for was *bigamy*. The darkness of her conscience and her scheming mind had left her with an inappropriate way of thinking. She was a witch on a broomstick, with no sense of direction.

Gail seemed to have great concern about Robert's well-being. Gail had Robert's back, in everything he did. In the hospital or on the highway, Gail was there. But at times, her character had her playing the role of both of his wives and living in the shadows of his past. At times he started to visualize and live the episodes of his previous marriages. Gail wanted a big wedding, since she had never been married before. And he promised her he would give her the wedding she wanted.

But after a while, Robert started to get cold feet at the thought of having a big wedding, because of all the drama in the little town they lived in. He was feeling very exhausted with all the rumors. He just wanted a quiet, simple wedding. But when he heard what Gail had told her sister, he got the impression it was her way or no way. He was reminded of his first wife, trying to take charge and disgracing him in front of her relatives. When she told him what she had told her sister, his mind snapped. He turned silent, saying to himself, *I guess it will be no way.*

He felt that her way of thinking wasn't in his best interest. He felt it was something they should have sat down to negotiate, because in a marriage, both of them needed to be on one accord. And also, Robert couldn't help seeing a side of Mary in her.

If Gail didn't like a female at the place of employment where they both worked, she would get upset with Robert if he talked to them simply out of courtesy, saying, "Good morning, how are you doing?"

And many days, in his presence, it was all right for other male coworkers to give her a neck-and-shoulder massage, and Robert never showed an attitude, because he trusted her. Again, he found himself in an atmosphere of "Do as I say, not as I do." His mind would drift. She wanted to hold a title with a different name, and he wanted a wife with a different attitude.

Gail was so used to being a single woman and doing things her own way. Even though if he was her husband, he was left with no room to guide her. She was being very hardheaded and disobedient and had no place for him in their marriage. The words she had spoken at the beginning when he first met her, that she was going to be obedient to her husband was a picture she had drawn, that couldn't be painted.

Again, in Robert's subconscious mind, *marriage* was a word that reminded him of his past. The abuse, cheating, and lying had left an imprint in his mind that gave him flashbacks of no returns. His mind drifted: A child may put their hands on a hot stove the first time. The second time, he would look at a distance, to avoid getting burned again. The imprint in the child's mind of the hot stove is now a no-no.

Gail was definitely a daddy's girl. She would ask Robert for his advice, but always had to confirm whatever Robert would say with her daddy. She would always say, "Daddy said this" or "Daddy said that," leaving him with the sobering thought that if he married her, he would be marrying her and her daddy. And nothing in their relationship was private. With Gail, there was no such thing as privacy. She would have been a good news reporter.

Gail's worst enemy was her own mouth, intimidating others of what she was going to do to them, finding herself trampled on because of her own words. Nevertheless, Gail was kind and had a pure heart that loved Robert in spite of all his faults. Truly, Gail's pure heart accepted him for who he was and not what she wanted him to be. But Gail's jealousy was like a water faucet that she felt she could turn on and off anytime she wanted to. In fact, their relationship was turned more off than on.

Gail reminded Robert so much of Mary, except Gail's mind wasn't filled with thoughts of material things she could gain. But her jealousy was an instrument that was setting her up to self-destruct. Marriage was a provision in Gail's mind that left Robert in the shadows of his past and a word that still wasn't in his vocabulary.

CHAPTER 14

Court

IRST OF ALL, YOU WILL be introduced to what is called a financial affidavit, which will give the court an overview of your income, your debts, and your expenses, and the kids involved in the marriage. The financial affidavit is a magnifying glass that puts all your income, debts, and expenses in plain view for the court.

Mary's attorney also requested something that was called a request for procurement.

The request was as follows:

* * *

1. A true and correct copy of any Federal and State Income Tax Returns in which you have an interest, personal and business, including all exhibits, schedule, and attachments and W-2 forms,

as intended to be or actually filed with the proper taxing agency for the period of the last four years.

2. All records and statement of any and all bank and financial assets or accounts, including checking, savings, money market, etc., account in existence for the past four years, including any and all bank books, records of deposits and withdrawals, monthly statements, check registers, and canceled checks on any such assets or accounts you or your spouse have any interest in of any kind or nature. Also please include documentation for all such assets identified on your affidavit of assets and liabilities as required to be filed by local rule.

3. Any and all records of any safe deposit box in which you or your spouse have an interest, whether solely or held jointly with any other person, together with a list of the contents contained therein.

4. Any and all of your payroll or paycheck stubs for the current year from your employment.

5. Any and all records of any income from any source other than your current employment for the past four years. Also include all records regarding to self-employment income, tips, cash payments, etc., regarding said income.

6. Any and all documents you have available to you evidencing your interest in savings bonds, certificates of deposit, and any and all financial assets in which you or your spouse have any interest, and which is not disclosed on paragraph two above.

7. Any and all life insurance policies now in effect or in effect within the past four years owned by either party, including all account statements evidencing the cash surrender value and loan value thereof for said four years' time period.

8. Any and all records with regard to any stocks, bond, mutual fund shares, money market account, or any other financial accounts in which you or your spouse have had any interest in the past four years, either vested or non-vested, and which were not disclosed in either paragraph two or paragraph six above.

9. Any and all records of any real property owned by you or your spouse, in either party's sole or joint names, or in any form of common ownership with any other person, including any form of land trust, and all documents evidencing ownership, title,

purchase, or the value thereof. Please include all documents regarding the purchase of same, including closing documents if available.

10. Any and all records of any indebtedness of any kind or nature of the parties, with individually or in joint names, including monthly statements for the four years.

11. Any and all financial statements given by either party to any bank or lending institution within the last four years.

12. Certificates of title to all motor vehicles, including but not limited to automobiles, trucks, boats, travel trailers, campers, motorcycles and licensable vehicles of any kind which either party owns or claims to have had an interest in over the last four years.

13. All records regarding and retirement and pension benefit programs, 401k or similar retirement programs either held individually by the parties or with any employer or private firm, owned by either party or in which either party has any interest.

14. A listing of any and all employee benefits including nature of the benefit, cost of the benefit, and who is covered by said benefits.

15. A true and correct verified Affidavit of Asset and Liabilities as required by Local Rule.

You are required pursuant to Amended Supreme Court 214 to produce the above requested documents as they are kept in the usual course of business or organized and labeled to correspond with the categories in this Request, including to produce all retrievable information in computer storage in printed form. Failure to organize the documents as required under Amended Court Rule 219.

You are further required pursuant to Amended Supreme Court Rule 214 to furnish an Affidavit whether the production is complete in accordance with this request, and if not complete, to list items not produced, stating the grounds for objection, and giving the names and addresses of persons having possession of such items.

Finally, pursuant to Amended Supreme Court Rule 214, you have an obligation to seasonably supplement your response to this Request to Produce by producing updated documents as they come into your possession or control, or become known to you, subsequent to your response to this Request.

＊　＊　＊

Upon Robert's first court appearance, Mary's attorney and his attorney waited in the hallways, patiently waiting for Mary's arrival. Later, her attorney informed his attorney that she wouldn't be able to attend court today and that another court date would be set.

In the back of Robert's mind, he knew she was afraid to attend because of her social security benefit and her under-the-table dealings with her own business, and her failure to report her income to Social Security.

Then again, he wondered if she had changed her mind and decided to stick with their verbal agreement. Later that same night, he met with her, hoping to learn that she didn't appear because she had decided not to pursue their divorce by fighting it out in court.

She approached him with great concern of the court finding out about her business, and she asked him why he was trying to hurt her. He assured her it wasn't his intention to hurt her at all, and that her having her own business was no concern of the court to a certain degree. The court was not trying to pursue her for having her own business and the fact that she was getting social security as well, but to determine what she was entitled to according to the law.

He explained to her that he would never do anything to hurt her. She carried on as though she was asking him for mercy, to not let the court know about her business. Little did he know she was testing the waters before she jumped in. And what he had just told her gave her the green light to unfold her scheming mind with her underhanded dealings.

A short time after, he received a letter from his attorney regarding another court hearing date because of Mary failing to appear for the first court hearing. He thought again that she might not appear in court because of her fear overpowering her greed. The date of the court hearing, he arrived and sat quietly looking down the hallway, hoping she wouldn't appear.

A short time later, her attorney arrived, and so did his attorney. Still, there was no Mary. Minutes later, she finally appeared, walking slowly down the hallway, ignoring him, as though he was a total stranger. The woman who had just passed him by—he didn't know her at all. She went down the hall where her attorney was sitting and never looked back.

Finally, their case was called in front of the judge. Robert sat quietly while Mary was called to take the stand. Her first attempt was getting the court to have sympathy for her medical condition and how she was unable to work. She also made it known that she had to pay for her medication. She was also terrified while she was on the stand. Her light bill was over a thousand dollars, and it was due.

She informed the court of Robert's lawn care business, perjuring herself by testifying he had more equipment than what he really did have. He sat there quietly, in a state of shock, knowing where she was trying to take this matter in the presence of the judge. Her attorney immediately asked the judge to award her maintenance and back pay maintenance as well. Robert just quietly sat there, bewildered by Mary's greed after he had given her what she wanted according to their verbal agreement.

When Robert's attorney cross-examined Mary on the stand, she presented the court with one of Mary's flyers for her own business. She immediately stated that the flyer was not hers, that Robert made it himself. Robert also gave his attorney Mary's client's names, addresses, and phones numbers and her income in black and white, in her own handwriting. She tried to deny the whole thing, but her record book of her clients' names and addresses and her income in her own handwriting made it hard for her to deny the truth.

Robert's attorney also informed the court about the newspaper article that one of her clients had written about her, in reference to her business. Mary denied the newspaper article as well, but the article spoke for itself.

She immediately looked at him, and her eyes seemed to be saying, *You said you weren't going to hurt me.* She actually wanted him to sit there helpless while she put herself in the spotlight and snatched what she could from him. Her reaction on the stand said he was doing her an injustice by overpowering her greed.

She also had evidence of his lawn care business, showing one of his flyers. His attorney informed the judge that Mary didn't deserve back pay because she didn't make her appearance on the first day of their court hearing.

Finally, the closing of their first day in court ended rather fast, and then they waited for the judge's decision, whether he was going to award her maintenance, and whether he had to pay her back pay. Right after court, Robert's attorney informed him the judge would notify him of his decision, and she in turn would notify Robert by mail.

Mary's attorney wanted the judge to award her temporary maintenance immediately, until the court decided what she was entitled to. But Robert knew that the evidence he had presented in court so far would make it hard for the judge to award her any maintenance at the present time until all the evidence had been brought forth. With no doubt, he knew he had put her and her attorney on the rope, and his intention was to keep them there.

After a couple weeks had passed, he finally received a letter from his attorney for the time being regarding the judge's decision, which denied her maintenance at the present time. The judge's decision gave Robert more energy to continue to do his homework, to keep the judge from reversing his decision. He would come home after working twelve hours or more, getting only a few hours of sleep, putting more evidence together in his defense, refusing to put his life in his attorney's hands.

He retrieved a big portion of her canceled checks that her clients had written her for her services in reference to her business, to show that her business did exist. He also noticed that all activities had ceased in the bank account he had set up for her. But it was too late for that; the damage had already been done. She still kept the account open with a small balance.

Nevertheless, she put her sandbags down after the flood. By the account being in his name, he was able to request all its activities and all the canceled checks she had deposited. Along with that, he did research on Medicare to block her attorney from coming at him with the COBRA law. All this information he retrieved, along with her clients' canceled checks, which he gave to his attorney.

Her brother and her sister-in-law were feeding him information on all of her bragging and intentions, and how she had confidence she was getting maintenance, and how hard her attorney was working to ensure that she would get maintenance. Her sister-in-law said to him that Mary wasn't going to walk out of that court without anything. Her attorney was doing his homework. But little did she know he was doing his homework as well, and she and her attorney were going to be surprised.

Upon their next court appearance, it was Robert's turn to take the stand. He could tell her attorney wasn't pleased at all about the judge's decision denying her maintenance. On the stand, Robert stated that Mary testified before the court that she was sick. He then replied, "I am sick as well and had document to support my statement."

He was once diagnosed with bladder cancer about six years ago, but it wasn't life-threatening, although he still had to see his doctor every year for a follow-up. He called his doctor's office and requested a written document stating he was under his care for a bladder cancer, which was the truth. And he had all the documents in his possession, from his entire doctor's visit, no matter how large, no matter how small.

Mary's attorney also asked Robert if he had any knowledge of Mary's sickness before he married her. Robert replied, "No, sir, I didn't." He knew that if he had said yes, then he had accepted her sickness before marrying her; therefore it would have been more of Robert's responsibility to take care her. And the judge would have taken that into consideration.

SUBPOENA

A subpoena was served to the human resources personnel at Robert's job to testify before the court of his earnings and benefits. And the subpoena stated YOU ARE COMMANDED ALSO to bring the following in your possession or control: Any and all reports and personnel records including, but not limited to, wage summary, time sheets, medical excuses, hour wage, etc., pertaining the named individual: Robert Smith.

The human resources personnel was called to the stand. Basically, Mary's attorney verified his hourly wages and his overtime and his benefits, and then the court released her from the stand.

Her attorney started on Robert's lawn care business, and he presented the court a picture of what he called Robert's lawn care trailer. Her attorney asked Robert on the stand if the trailer in the picture was his trailer.

He replied, "No, sir, the trailer you see in the picture is my son's trailer." His son's name was the same as his, but his son was the IV, and the registration for the trailer displayed the *IV* as well. He also stated how Mary had given him information about his lawn care business, and how he was also certified with the Department of Transportation.

Robert sat up straight, staring Mary's attorney in the eyes, and asked, "Did she inform you of this as well?" He pulled out the ad he had placed in the newspaper months before he had left her, an ad she had no knowledge of. The newspaper ad stated, "Going out of business, equipment for sale, must sell."

The newspaper ad was used as a document in court. Robert said, "Yes, I was certified with the Department of Transportation at one time but never generated one penny of an income from them."

Afterward he was cross-examined by his own attorney, who asked him, "When you sold your equipment, did you sell everything, even your weed eaters?"

Robert replied, "Yes, I did."

He was cross-examined again by Mary's attorney about his financial affidavit, how his debts could exceed his income. He replied, "My affidavit is correct. That's what I am trying to get across to you and the court."

Robert could feel the tension and the frustration of her attorney, and he thought it was getting a little personal, because every punch her attorney threw was blocked. He observed Mary sitting in the courtroom, whispering in her attorney's ear, as though she was helping him come at him from a different angle. She would glance at him on the stand with a scheming, sneaky smile, trying to get herself and her attorney off the ropes. He just chuckled to himself, saying, *You better leave well enough alone because my heavy artillery is yet to come.*

Later, the divorce hearing was postponed for another day. Still, no maintenance was granted.

Robert had analyzed Mary and her attorney's strategy of dragging their divorce out in court to reach the ten-year mark, legally binding her to his retirement. He had separated from her going over the ninth year, and a few months more would put them in their tenth year of marriage.

Robert tried to get his attorney to try to push the judge to finalize his divorce before his tenth year of marriage to Mary. But he also knew he couldn't just focus on that alone, because he had so many other things on his plate, such as blocking her from getting maintenance for a lifetime and blocking the COBRA law as well.

From the first day of court, Mary had perjured herself in court and Robert's next task was to put her in the spotlight, making her lose her credibility in court.

Upon their next court appearance, Mary's attorney painted an image of Robert as a playboy who was still having an affair with Mary. She had a female friend of Robert's subpoenaed to testify that she was having an affair with him.

Mary's attorney refused to put her on the stand after she told what was going on. Robert's friend didn't know what Mary was talking about and denied having any affair with him. The subpoena was served along with a twenty-five-dollar check for her to appear and for her expenses.

Mary's attorney didn't care about the expense because he figured it was being added to Mary's attorney's fee, leaving Robert to pay it. He also made an attempt to serve Gail a subpoena, along with another twenty-five-dollar check, but was unable to do so. Mary's attorney thought he was running up his attorney fees to put more expenses on Robert.

Robert saw the humor in this, and he chuckled to himself. He hoped her attorney would send him a twenty-five-dollar check as well, which would give him more willpower, for the bomb Mary's attorney had set for Robert would blow up in Mary's hands, leaving her holding the bag.

As Mary took the stand, Robert passed his attorney a copy of her present light bill, which they brought up after Mary had testified to the court that her light bill was over a thousand dollars. Upon cross-examining her, Robert's attorney asked her again, how much was her light bill?

Mary replied, "Over a thousand dollars."

Robert's attorney said, "Here, I see your light bill has a zero balance."

She had perjured herself once again. She looked at Robert as though, she was going to faint and needed CPR. Her attorney knew they had taken another big blow of defeat. Slowly but surely, she was losing her credibility in the judge's eyes based on the evidence Robert had prepared. Robert couldn't help but think Mary's attorney must be wondering, *Who is this man?*

Mary was asked to step down from the stand after his attorney had finished cross-examining her. Robert was then asked by Mary's attorney to take the stand.

He went back to the early part of the court hearing, beginning to cross-examine Robert on something he had testified to, as well as trying to highlight Robert's credibility. Robert stated on the stand, "Sir, you are trying to confuse me on the stand, and you, sir, are confusing yourself. Mr Robert Smith never said no such thing, but what I did say was this." And Robert quoted what he had said.

Mary's attorney also came at him in reference to his daughter, of what he had put on his affidavit about her allowance and her hairdresser. Robert replied, "By my daughter being a female and by me being a man.

When it came to her personal needs, she might feel a little embarrassed to ask me for certain things. Instead of embarrassing her, I make sure she has enough money to take care of her personal needs. And yes, I do pay what I said on my financial affidavit for her hairdresser."

Court was postponed again, and no maintenance was granted.

By now, Mary's frustration was beginning to show. Since the car she was driving was in Robert's name, she began to get parking tickets and holding them until they reached the maximum amount. And then she would mail them to Robert in a business-type envelope with no return address, to make it seem as though the city had mailed him the tickets. He mailed the tickets to her, and she mailed them back to him.

He didn't hesitate paying the tickets because the car was in his name, although it gave him another tool to fight with, showing she was incompetent enough for the car to be in his name. And besides, he had withdrawn cash out of the checking account that he had set up for her business. And then he had deposited the cash in his checking account and paid the parking tickets with her own money, using one of his personal checks, showing the court evidence that he had paid the tickets.

Needless to say, she stopped paying her car note and had gotten about two months behind, trying to put pressure on him by trying to ruin his credit. Robert put together her payment history, and he knew he had to convince the court that her past due payments weren't because she wasn't able to pay it but, instead, was for revenge.

A short time later, Robert received a letter from his attorney concerning a settlement offer from Mary's attorney. The offer was as follows:

> In order to resolve this case, be advised that Ms. Mary Smith wants half of the pension and retirement benefits that he has accumulated during the marriage. Half of the proceeds from the sale of his lawn equipment, maintain medical insurance for the period of 18 months, payment of car insurance until the car is paid off, all outstanding attorney fees and $300.00 per month for maintenance for 18 months.

Robert called his attorney and informed her that he was refusing Mary's attorney's offer, but that he wanted her to tell Mary's attorney to go to hell. He just chuckled at Mary's attorney wanting half of his lawn care proceeds, when the newspaper ad was placed during the marriage and the money was used as marital asset to pay their debts. And it was hard for Mary's attorney to prove otherwise.

An earlier court date was arranged to address the parking tickets on her vehicle and the past due amount that she refused to pay. Upon review of her payment history, it could be seen that she never had been late, up until the time Robert had left her. The judge asked Mary why she was behind on her payment, and she replied she didn't know. She was hesitant to answer, not knowing what Robert had up his sleeve. She didn't want to perjure herself again on the stand; she was scared of underestimating his expectations in the courtroom by now.

Then the judge asked her if she could pay the two car notes that were overdue. Mary didn't know whether Robert could prove that she could pay it. He had gotten her too paranoid to perjure herself again in the judge's eyes. She replied, "Yes, I can pay it." The judge gave her only a few days to pay both notes, or she had to give the car back to Robert.

The tickets she had gotten were addressed as well. Mary's attorney asked her why she didn't pay the ticket, and she replied she didn't have the money at the time.

After that, Robert's attorney cross-examined her. She pointed out to Mary that it wasn't Robert's responsibility to pay her tickets when she was the driver of the vehicle. Looking at the expression on the judge's face, Robert could tell he knew Mary was lying and had perjured herself again.

Mary then stepped down off the stand. She had started whining on the stand, saying, "He said if I needed him, he would be there for me."

Robert smiled, thinking, *She's not lying now. She doesn't have the money now.* This after he had withdrawn the money out of her own checking balance to pay the parking ticket, leaving a zero balance, closing the account. Robert's least worry was her exposing him for what he had done, because she didn't want the court to find out about her checking account for her business.

Robert's attorney put him on the stand and asked him about his opinion on Mary driving a car in his name and being irresponsible behind the wheel. He stated, "Without my CDL, I don't have a job, and she has my whole career in the palm of her hand."

Mary's bitterness had grown to a level where she had to destroy him in any way she knew how, and knowing that now their relationship would be bruised forever. At the end of the court hearing, the trial was postponed again, *with no maintenance granted.*

Robert knew he had to clear up all doubts in the judge's mind about her business and prove his business really didn't exist.

Robert had Mary's brother and his wife subpoenaed, knowing neither one wanted to take his side because of the hardship it would cause Mary, but with what he had in mind, their testimony would be in his favor before they realized what had happened. He also remembered Mary informed one of her clients she wasn't able to clean her house anymore due to being overloaded with clients, so he had this client subpoenaed too.

Upon their next court appearance, Mary and her attorney had knowledge of him having her brother and his wife subpoenaed, but had no knowledge at all about one of her clients having been subpoenaed to testify. Since Robert had hired her brother to work with him in his lawn care business and his wife had knowledge of this as well, could play a major role that his business no longer existed.

Robert's attorney asked him who he wanted to take the stand first, Mary's brother or his wife, and he said to put Mary's sister-in-law on the stand first. Then she asked him what he wanted her to ask her. He said to his attorney, "Ask her, did her husband work with me in my lawn care business? And when was the last time he worked in my lawn care business?"

"First question: did your husband work with Robert in his lawn care business?"

Mary's sister-in-law replied, "Yes, he did."

"Second question: when was the last time he worked with Robert in his lawn care business?"

"Oh, it's been well over a year."

Robert chuckled, saying to himself, *She just closed the door of a business that no longer existed.*

In a low voice, Robert's attorney asked him, was there anything else he wanted her to ask Mary's sister-in-law? Robert replied that she had just testified in his favor and didn't even realize she had. She then asked him if he wanted to put Mary's brother on the stand. He replied, "There's no need to. His wife just testified for them both."

Upon informing Mary's sister-in-law that she could step down from the stand, Robert's attorney called one of Mary's old client to the stand.

Mary's attorney objected at once on the ground that no one informed him of another witness, and that he wasn't prepared and asked for this hearing to be postponed.

Mary looked at Robert as if to say, *What are you doing to me?* The judge asked Mary's attorney, "Since when did another attorney have to inform you of their witness?"

He replied, "Judge, it's just a courtesy." Mary's attorney's request for a postponement was denied.

Mary's client Rose Wilson took the stand. Ms. Wilson was asked, was she a client of Mary's? She said she used to be, but not anymore. Robert's attorney asked why she said "used to be." She said Mary had told her she wouldn't be able to clean her house anymore because she had too many clients. Robert's attorney asked her how much she was paying Mary a month. Ms. Wilson said about four hundred a month. Robert's attorney then said to the court that she had no more questions.

Mary's attorney cross-examined Ms. Wilson and asked her if she and Robert at any time discussed this case." She replied, "No, we didn't." He then said it was hard for him to believe. She was paying her four hundred dollars a months. Her reply was, "Yes, I was."

He then asked her as well, "Who are you having to clean your house now?"

Ms. Wilson looked at the judge and said, "That's my business." And then she asked the judge if she had to answer the question. The judge looked at Mary's attorney and replied, "No, she doesn't have to answer that question." The court once again scheduled another hearing, and *no maintenance was granted.*

Robert knew that deep down in Mary's guts, she really did hate him. A long, drawn-out divorce she thought was a dream was now turning out to be her worst nightmare. At the beginning of this divorce, he couldn't even visualize her disheartened, with a dark shadow on her spiritual beliefs, leaving his mind filled with distrust. She had flushed her spiritual beliefs right down the toilet for greed, hoping to gain the material things that life had to offer and selling out her soul.

Robert's thoughts drifted, mentally calling Mary the princess of evil. Nevertheless, he knew he still had to brace himself since he did not know her next move. Her narrow mind was unstoppable; she would betray everything she believed in and everything that stood in her way. After all they had been through in court, she was still telling people the judge was going to award her maintenance upon her next court appearance. She was in denial and didn't want anyone to know she was being ground down like a cheap piece of metal that soon wouldn't exist.

Her main concern was still about Robert talking to all those women. Her twisted thoughts were wedged deep down in her uncontrollable mind, and she refused to accept the word *defeat*. She had bragged to everyone she knew about how she was going to take Robert to the bank, and even worse, that she didn't want to be laughed at and ridiculed for being defeated. She was totally knocked senseless being persuaded by greed.

After months and months with a drawn-out divorce trial, the end was getting very near, and what Mary and her attorney had up their sleeves wouldn't really surprise Robert at all. They were determined to win this case—a case that Robert felt was getting very personal, zeroing in on Robert's behavior and the way he held his own in court. He knew Mary's attorney pictured him as a smartass, which really did irritate him.

Upon their next court appearance, Robert was sitting in the hallway waiting for court to start when he noticed that one of Mary's brothers was there. At that time, he had no knowledge whether she had paid him to testify that he had seen Robert on his riding mower cutting one of his client's grass, and that his business still existed. Her greed had overruled her expectation, and her hate had overruled her sins.

Robert's attorney looked at him and asked him, "Who is that?" He informed his attorney that the man was Mary's brother, and later it was revealed that he was there to testify. He also informed her he was a felon, and that his credibility in court would weaken his testimony.

Mary's attorney started out introducing the court to what he called a value witness, to testify in behalf of Mary Smith. Mary's brother was called to the stand, and he testified that he saw Robert cutting grass on his riding mower, and gave the court the location of one of previous clients that Mary had knowledge of.

Mary's brother couldn't look Robert in the eye, because he knew Mary had paid him to perjure himself. After he had testified, Robert's attorney cross-examined him by asking him what his relation was to Mary.

"I am her brother."

Robert's attorney asked him if he was a felon, and he said, "Yes, I am."

Little did Mary know that a relative's testimony was good, it didn't carry a lot of weight. And her brother's being a felon was even worse. Right after Robert's attorney asked Mary's brother to step down, she called Robert to take the stand. She asked him, was Mary's brother's testimony the truth? Robert replied, no, it wasn't. And right after, Robert was cross-examined by Mary's attorney.

He started off by asking, "If you win this case, will you continue to pay Mary car insurance?"

Robert replied, "Mary has enough income to pay my insurance."

Filled with frustration, Mary's attorney said in a thundering voice, "Your Honor, make Mr. Smith answer the question."

Robert raised his voice and replied boldly, "Your Honor, I just did. He's not listening." He then continued, "No, I will not continue to pay her car insurance. She is able to pay it on her own."

What Mary's attorney wanted was a commitment from Robert. If she lost the case, the judge could take under consideration that Robert testified he would continue to pay her car insurance. After Robert made his statement, the judge immediately said, "Recess."

As Robert stepped down from the stand and walked into the hallway, Robert's attorney said, "You are letting her attorney have it in there," as if to say, *You are making her attorney look bad in front of the judge.*

In Robert's mind, if a man wasn't standing up for what he believed in, then how could he stand up for what was right, always being afraid to face the shadows of his past? And being nice to a snake would leave you totally off guard for it to bite you.

After recess, Robert was called back to the stand by Mary's attorney. He seemed to be exhausted and very disoriented, scratching his head, not knowing how to come at Robert with the next question, and not certain what his next move would be. His mind was completely blank. The court got so quiet for a few seconds. You could actually hear the sound of a pin drop. Everyone had their eyes on Mary's attorney, waiting for his next move, but still he was totally speechless.

without of frustration, he said, "Your Honor, Mary Smith wants half of Robert's retirement." This after he had drawn out the case long enough to meet the ten-year mark, binding Mary legally to Robert's retirement. Robert was still on the stand at the time.

Robert said, "Judge, if you can recall, I testified at the beginning of this trial that Mary and I had a verbal agreement, and when I left, I left her everything we had agreed on, which have more value than my retirement at the time.

"However, I am not denying my retirement is a marital asset, but everything I left behind was marital asset as well. If she wants half of my retirement, then I would like half of everything I left behind." For a moment, Robert's mind drifted in a deep thought. Mary was like a thief in the night, trying to take everything without his consent.

Mary's attorney also stated that she was seeking to keep her health insurance under the COBRA law. Right after that, Robert's attorney cross-examined Mary in reference to the value of their marital asset and the value of what Robert had left behind, bringing up that what he had left behind had greater value. After another hearing, there was *still no maintenance granted*.

A short time after court, one of Mary's brothers informed Robert that Mary had paid her stepbrother to testify, perjuring himself, giving him little of nothing, because he had a drug addiction. Mary had taken advantage of her own brother's sickness.

She was a rattlesnake, and ready to strike; and the only way he could keep her from biting him was to hold her head, because her expectations of winning had no limitation. But only if she and her attorney knew that he still had even more evidence of her being employed. Not once did he expose all of her canceled checks that her clients had paid her. He was still holding back.

The more her attorney drew out the trial, the more he was putting her in quicksand; and the more they wiggled, the deeper they sank. A week or two later, Robert received a letter from his attorney requesting document from his employer indicating the cost of keeping Mary covered with her health insurance under the COBRA law. Even from day one, he had done everything her attorney had asked of him, giving her attorney no ground for defense. Immediately, he went to gather the information her attorney requested.

After Robert had received the information Mary's attorney requested, he reviewed the amount it would cost to keep her covered, but the cost would come out of his pocket. Under the COBRA law, Mary's insurance would cost him over $800 a month. He actually felt her attorney's anger over his actions. But being threatened by her attorney was the least of his worries.

Robert knew it was time for him to do his homework, to throw a wrench once again in Mary and her attorney's work. He was going to give her and her attorney a rude awakening, shattering their confidence that they could keep him under their thumb and go unpunished for the abuse she had put his daughters through. Robert would give her something to remember.

The times Robert was stepping on her and her attorney, he was thinking, *Bitch, this is for my daughters.* He was using his anger as a level tool to stay on course to defeat her. And his actions that she would see in court would be the anger he had kept bottled within

Robert would be a man not claiming to be smart, but a man who loved his kids; and with all of his power, he was going to beat her without any physical contact. A bruise would sooner or later heal, but destroying her heart, her mind, and her greed would last longer, leaving her with a scar that she would remember for the rest of her life.

CHAPTER 15

The End of a Long and Nasty Court Battle

MARY'S RUDENESS AND HER DEVILISH ways would be planted in her mind, not only today but also in the years to come. And Robert's name would be the name branded in her mind, and she would be cursing his mother for his birth, and she would be calling him a son of a bitch. Theirs was a premeditated divorce that would leave her branded for life. However, Robert put in all his effort to defeat her, which left him with no conflicting emotions that included pity. Nevertheless, feeling like an exhausted fighter by the twelfth round, he must answer to the bell, to knock her out.

And from the beginning to the end of his divorce trial, Robert's inch-thick evidence binder was now over three inches thick, containing information from the time of Mary's birth to the present, even the things she had lived and had forgotten about, he had them in the binder. He had isolated her entire life at his fingertip in a three-inch binder. He took nothing for granted, having prepared himself for any subject that would be brought up in court. He was prepared to go the distance. He had to laugh at himself, thinking the only thing he didn't know was her blood type.

Robert knew he had a really good attorney to help him achieve his goal, but he simply refused to just put his life in the palm of any attorney's hand, not without putting up a good fight for himself. Many nights his crowded mind wouldn't let him rest, as he gathered more and more evidence to win his case. He did not know Mary and her attorney's next task, but one thing was for sure: he knew the anger he had would be left behind in the courtroom.

He knew Mary's attorney's next subject was the COBRA law, and that he had assured her they would win. Robert could picture her in his mind, laughing at him. And her attorney saying, "Oh well, we got you now."

A short time later, Robert received a date for the last court hearing that would finalize his divorce from Mary once and for all. Undoubtedly, a decision would be made based on the evidence that had been brought forth to the court, and the decision would be reinforced by the court's findings.

Now the crucial day had arrived, and once again, he sat patiently in the hallway, across the hall from the courtroom doors, waiting patiently until his name was called. And again, he watched Mary walk down the hall, as calm as she could be, to meet with her attorney.

As the court assembled, Robert's attorney called Mary to the stand. She started on her health insurance, and Mary denied having any other health insurance than the health insurance she had from Robert's employer. Robert's lawyer said, "And earlier in the trial, you testified having to co-pay."

Then she asked Mary about her Medicare card, raising a copy of her Medicare for the whole court to view. And from Robert's research, she read the evidence he had prepared in reference to Mary's Medicare prescription drug coverage. It read as follows: "Medicare prescription drug coverage is available to everyone with Medicare, regardless of income, health status, or how you pay for prescription drugs today."

Mary rolled her eyes; she looked as though she was getting ready to pass out on the stand. Robert's attorney asked, "You mean to tell me you never received this information in the mail?"

Mary stumbled over her words. "I . . . I . . . I did but didn't understand what it meant." Again she had lied; perjury just wasn't her best friend. Robert knew that at this point, her credibility had just gone down the drain. During the time she was on the stand, Robert glanced at her attorney, and he looked as though he had just lost his best friend.

Robert's attorney told Mary that she could step down from the stand. Immediately, Mary's attorney called Robert to the stand. He kept staring at the copy of Mary's medical card that Robert had provided his attorney. Mary's attorney knew Robert had just successfully blocked him from seeking the COBRA law. Once again, her attorney knew Robert had thrown another punch that kept them pinned against the ropes.

Mary's attorney would look at Robert and then at Mary's Medicare card, shaking his head, shifting his eyes back and forth. And all the while, he had an argumentative attitude. "Where did you get this from?" he asked, holding Mary's Medicare card in his hand.

Robert replied, "It doesn't matter where I got it from. The facts remain I got it. And the evidence speaks for itself."

Mary's attorney then stated, "You must have got it when you came by to see her."

Robert started to say, "Your Honor, I reject that statement. He is trying to lead the plaintiff," but instead, he glanced at the man with a faint smile. Mary's attorney was filled with so much frustration. He knew Robert had just protected himself from the COBRA law.

Robert's mind drifted for a moment as he sat quietly, wondering what Mary and her attorney were thinking, how they had underestimated his expectations, of the role he was playing in court. And even if he didn't win, he would have left an imprint of a condemned man fighting for his life.

From the beginning to the end of the trial, Robert's whole attitude had been concentrated with boldness, refusing to be Mary's and her attorney's puppet on a string. Don't throw any mud if you don't want any to be thrown back at you. And they both left a muddy mess. They threw many punches but forgot to block. The look Mary and her attorney gave

Robert was filled with frustration. If looks could kill, Robert would have been dead and embalmed before he could leave the stand.

Afterward, Robert was asked to step down, and both attorneys went over their closing arguments. And after the closing arguments, the judge still didn't make his decision. Each party would be notified by their attorneys by mail of the judge's verdict.

CHAPTER 16

The Judge's Verdict at the End of the Tunnel and The Dissolution of a Marriage

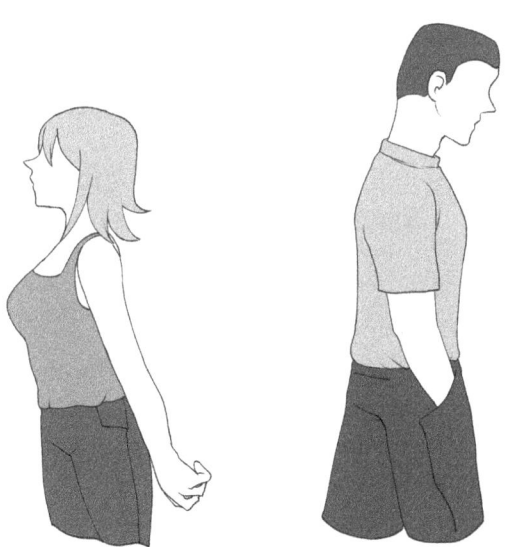

THIS CAUSE IS HEARD ON the Petition for Dissolution of Marriage of the Petitioner, Robert Smith, who is present personally and by his Attorney Betty Jameson; the Respondent, Mary Smith by her attorney Jerome Whitmore and the Court having heard the evidence and arguments the Court, having full knowledge of basis on the above captioned proceeding, and having considered all evidence relative to it:

FIND THAT;

1. This Court has Jurisdiction of the parties and of subject matter of this proceeding.
2. The Petitioner has proven the material allegations of the petition for Dissolution by substantial, competent, and relevant evidence; and this judgment should, accordingly, be entered.
3. At the commencement of this action, the parties were residents in the State, which they both lived, and such residence has been maintained for at least ninety days next preceding and making these findings.
4. The parties were married on July 13, 1997, and said marriage was registered in the County where they lived.
5. The parties have irreconcilable differences and grounds have been by competent evidence.
6. There were no children of the marriage. The wife is not now pregnant and no children have been adopted by the parties.

ACCORDINGLY, IT IS HEREBY ORDERED AND ADJUDGED THAT:

I. GENERAL

1. The parties are awarded a Judgment of Dissolution of Marriage, and the marriage of the parties is terminated and dissolved.
2. Any right, claim. Or interest of the parties in the property of the other, whether real, personal or mixed, of whatever kind and nature and wherever situated, including, but not limited to, homestead, succession, and inheritance, arising out of marital relationship or any other relationship existing between the parties, except as expressly set forth above and is forever barred and terminated.
3. Each of the parties will, promptly upon demand by the other party or as otherwise provided for n herein shall execute and deliver to effectuate and fulfill the term of this judgment.
4. The court expressly retains jurisdiction of this cause and the parties for the purpose of modifying or enforcing all the terms of

judgment or other supplementary procedures consistent with the State Marriage and Dissolution of Marriage Act.

II. PROPERTY

1. Personal Property. Except as provided herein each party is awarded the personal property and furnishing in their possession. Except as may otherwise be provided, each party shall be responsible for indebtedness on property to which that party is entitled, and each party shall indemnify and hold the other party harmless on any such indebtedness.
2. Pension. Robert Smith is awarded as his own pension offered through his employment.
3. Bank Accounts. The parties are awarded their own personal saving and checking accounts.
4. Vehicles. The wife shall keep as her own the 2005 Toyota and she be solely responsible for any indebtedness due thereon. Mary is granted forty-five days to refinance the car and if she fails to do so she must return the car to Robert for him to sell and Mary shall receive the net proceeds. The husband shall have as his own all other vehicles and shall be solely liable for the indebtedness due therein. Each shall hold the other harmless thereon awarded them and sign vehicle titles necessary to effect the terms of the Judgment.
5. Nonmarital Property. Each party shall keep his or her own non marital property, clothing, jewelry and personal items.

III. MAINTENANCE

1. Maintenance is denied and it is forever barred.

IV. DEBTS AND LIABILITIES

1. The Petitioner shall assume the remaining marital debt which is listed in his affidavit of approximately $4,300.00.
2. Payment of Debts. Except as otherwise provided for herein each party agrees to pay and be responsible for all other personal debts and obligations which he or she has incurred in their own name

or will incur, and further shall hold the other party harmless for all such personal debts and obligations.

V. ATTORNEY'S FEES

Robert Smith shall reimburse Mary $ 1,000.00 toward her attorney fees. All other requests for attorney fees are denied.

* * *

And even before and after their divorce, Mary scandalized Robert's name, with gossip from one end of the town to the other—how he was trying to take her car from her, isolating the truth, of her getting parking ticket in the vehicle and mailing the tickets to him.

After Robert had read the dissolution of his marriage, his mind drifted. A person shouldn't live beyond their thoughts and beyond their expectations just for greed. Once again, he had left behind his past, leaving Mary with a future that would always be imprinted with defeat, cursing the grounds that Robert walked on. Actually, the fact remains: no one ever wins in a divorce. No attorney, no judge can play God Almighty and give you back the years that were wasted out of your life. One wasted day is one day too many.

Robert's attorney played a great part in Mary's defeat, being such a great attorney and mouthpiece, and conquering the legal aspects of his case. And Robert was very fortunate to have her in his corner. She was an attorney who wasn't too big-headed to listen. Robert's plans had been well executed.

CHAPTER 17

The Aftermath

THE JUDGE'S DECISION WAS BASED on facts, and Robert thanked God for the knowledge he had given him to defeat Mary in her devilish ways, and he gave God the praise for helping him know her heart, and to step on the things that stood against him, giving him the strength to conquer his enemies. Mary's sense of greed had overruled her senses, and Robert had channeled his anger at her for her abuses by using his documents as a tool to defeat her. Mary's greed had knocked her senseless. The things they had verbally agreed on. She beguiled him, instead she would rather gamble on the bird in the bush than the one in her hand.

Robert monitored Mary's car payment on his computer in order to know when it was OK to drop her car insurance. In less than a week, she had paid the car off, in cash. Her balance was approximately $ 12,000. At that point, he canceled her car warranty, receiving a refund of about $340, which he used for her attorney's fees. The total cost he paid for her attorney's fee was about $660. He just smiled, saying to himself, *Hope her car doesn't break down anytime soon.*

Robert immediately canceled the car insurance, but left the liability until he was sure the vehicle was out of his name. The very next day, she was in a car collision, and there was a confrontation with the other driver, not knowing who was in the wrong. She went right away to make a claim against Robert's insurance company to fix her vehicle, only to discover he had canceled her full coverage the day before, leaving her only with liability insurance. It seemed as though she was starting to pay for her devilish ways, with no pity from God.

Mary was steaming mad. If she was God, Robert would already have been dead and burning in hell. Right after she had paid in cash for her car, she was riding in something that looked as though it had been hit by an 18-wheeler. Weeks had passed before she finally got her car repaired. A short time later, Robert's cousin was at his apartment when a police officer knocked on the door, but Robert wasn't home. The officer left his phone number for Robert to call him.

The next day, while he was at work, Robert called the officer, who stated that Mary had made a police report accusing him of stealing her radio out of her vehicle and cutting up her seats. Robert explained to the officer that it was all an act of revenge, after he had just defeated her in court. Little did Mary know that Robert had given a spare set of keys to his attorney to give to her attorney, in exchange for her car keys, demanding his license plates that she had taken off her vehicle.

The police officer was very nice, asking Robert, did he commit such an act? And Robert replied, "No, I didn't." And then the officer said he could tell Mary was lying. She still hadn't done enough lying in court. Robert had his attorney to inform Mary's attorney that the next time she filed a false police report on him, he was pressing charges. And it wasn't a threat but a promise. And Robert couldn't help wondering, how could a person call themselves a child of God and be so evil-minded? Even after the divorce, Mary was still reaching out to torment him like an evil spirit from the past.

Robert chuckled to himself, thinking, years ago, this was a woman who had nothing and claiming to have a disability when he had made her the success she was today; and now she was trying to exert every effort to destroy him. Robert just thought it was a funny way for her to show her gratitude, proving to her and the court that she was no handicap, that she was capable of taking care of herself. It's a fact: some people you just can't help.

Needless to say, a guy named Frank stepped onto Robert's bus. Frank was a little intoxicated, but he knew Mary. In fact, he knew the whole family. He went on to say that Gail was a better woman than Mary. He said something about how he used to have sex with Mary and how she liked to be handcuffed and beaten during their sexual intercourse. He described her as a freak who loved pain. Yes, the little town was so small, but she had a reputation that made the town larger than it was.

Again, there was another passenger who boarded Robert's bus on another occasion. The passenger said that he was new in town. The conversation led to what church he was going to, and it was funny that he named Mary's church. He went on to say that he knew the usher of the church liked him, because she was always teasing him. He said her name was Mary. The man being new in town, Robert wasn't surprised at all by what he heard.

A new face was a target to hide her reputation that everyone else in town already knew. She had a web like a spider, catching men that weren't from her hometown, who knew nothing of her sexual activities.

A few months later, a coworker by the name of Anthony asked Robert for his attorney's name and her phone number, because he was filing for a divorce. He liked the outcome of Robert's case, and in his mind, Robert's attorney was the key he needed in his defense. It was a mystery to hear his case, which had the same scenario as Robert's.

His wife was on disability, and there were no kids involved in their divorce. Robert, being a low-profile person, did not wish to get involved if he was not invited. In a roundabout way, he would say, "Don't just depend on your attorney to win your case." Robert felt it wasn't his business if Anthony didn't ask for his advice. Somehow, Anthony gave Robert the impression he had everything under control.

From time to time, Robert would ask Anthony how his divorce case was going, and Anthony would always reply that it was going OK. For some reason, Robert felt Anthony was in a boat that would soon sink, with no life jacket within reach. Sad to say, Anthony was going under. He seemed to be filled with so much anger and just wanted out of his marriage. He had no plans and no strategy other than an attorney he was depending on to pull a rabbit out of her hat.

Robert badly wanted to tell him to use his anger as a level tool, but just by observing Anthony's behavior, Robert could tell his mind was made up to go on a journey that could affect him for the rest of his life. It hurt Robert to see a man drowning and all he could do was just stand there and watch him drown. Anthony's anger had taken a toll on him, knocking him senseless.

Anthony would just sit at work, trying to convince himself that the judge wasn't going to award his wife anything. He would say, "I told her she won't get anything." But unfortunately, Anthony wasn't the judge.

He put his whole life in the hands of an attorney. He knew Robert's attorney won his case, but he didn't have any knowledge of all the details involved in Robert's case.

Anthony, just like Robert, had a long and drawn-out case. But unfortunately, with the same attorney, Anthony was left with a nightmare that would affect him for the rest of his life. The judge awarded his wife maintenance for the rest of her life, along with half of Anthony's retirement.

Anthony ended up resigning from his job due to medical reasons. But whatever the real reasons why he resigned, he had to swallow a pill that was too big for him.

Many people in Robert's town applauded him on the outcome of his divorce case. He heard them say, "What had happened to you in your divorce case doesn't happen here in this town." What was even more amazing was that Robert found himself in somewhat of a daze, looking back at his odds of defeating Mary in court and what God had brought him out from. It seemed as though God himself was tapping him on his shoulder.

A young man who boarded Robert's bus approached him and told him in a very low voice, "I only have eighty cents, and I am twenty cents short of my fare." Robert acknowledged him with a subtle nod. Upon reaching the end of the bus line, the young man got off.

Robert stepped off the bus, and the young man walked up to him and said, "You are a believer, aren't you."

Robert replied, "Yes, I am."

The young man went on to say, "I just got out of prison, and yesterday, I went to church and was saved." And then he said, "Would you please pray for me?"

Robert couldn't see the young man's face with the hood he had over his head to ward off the cold.

The young man's face was buried so deep in the oversize hood that covered his head, and Robert could see only a dark shadow that covered his face. As Robert looked deep under the hood of the young man, he could see the tears running down his face. His eyes were red, as though he had been crying for a while.

The young man praised God in his own way, being sincere, and just hearing the young man's words really penetrated Robert's heart.

Robert replied, "I will pray for you, and you pray for me. I am seeking the same thing you are."

The young man went on to say that while he was in prison, he told God, *If you are the Father, which I say you are, then why can't I be a better son?*

Those words from the young man touched Robert's heart even more, as when he looked back, he could see where God had brought him from. In other words, what the young man was really saying was, *If I believe in you, like I say I do, then why can't I keep your commandments?*

The young man's words brought Robert back out of the shadows that God had already brought him out of.

Even more so, Robert gave praise to God. He was only an instrument that was highly favored by the Man Upstairs. From that day on, *God was still manifesting himself in Robert's life.*

* * *

The Prayer Of The Provision Of God's Will

O LORD, I THANK YOU FOR knowing the heart. When all doors were closed, you opened them. When many said I couldn't defeat her, you said, "Yes you can."

And, Lord, forgive me of all my daily doubts. Even I too, Lord, haven't always been good, but I thank you for your rain that rains on the just and the unjust, and your sun that shines as well. I thank you for the things you did and for the things you are going to do in my life.

And all the things she cased out on my kids and me, I never raised a hand on her or used any physical force—not my defeat but your defeat was manifested by my silence, and by my movements, just by standing still. You manifested yourself again when I left New Orleans on that Greyhound bus. You said you were with me all the way, and you would never leave me.

Lord, I have been from one end of this world to the next, and still to this day, you have kept your promise. Through all of my wrongs and my convictions, my trials and my tribulations, you still stood in the gap, and for your grace that carried me from the prayers of others who loved me so dearly. There were things the judge and the attorneys did not know. I was blessed and highly favored and was carried through the battlefield by the prayers of my father and my mother, who conquered the evil forces that stood before me.

O Lord, I thank you. Let every individual examine themselves of the faults they have within themselves, and let them not harden their hearts to the faults in others. I thank you for making me whole, for taking away the anger, the hate that hinders me, for restoring to me love and passion, for taking away the evil thoughts, for helping me leave the past in the courtroom. Lord, your words shall dwell within me, and like a bird, I will spread my wings and soar to reach higher grounds for the righteousness of the things that are pleasing to thee. Amen.

I went to visit my dentist, and just out of a conversation, we started to talk about divorce. He had been through his already, and I was already getting started to set in motion my own divorce proceedings. In fact, I already had in mind at the time the right attorney and how much money I would need to get myself out of this mess. He told me about how he had spent so much money for his attorney's fees. He told me about how he had wasted money on one attorney and had to get another. The dollars he had spent was in the thousands. Right then, what went through my head was I didn't have the kind of money he did; and if he lost his battle in court, I knew I would lose mine as well. Right then and there, I realized that depending on the power of the dollar and an attorney wasn't the key. I had to take a different approach.

This book wasn't written for a specific gender or race, but for anyone who feels he or she is trapped and sees no way out.

When I looked at all the angles and saw no open doors, no gaps, the odds being too much against me, I looked deep within myself and was introduced to my inner spirit, which was just waiting to take control. Anger was put on the side, because patience and planning were the key.

I had to clear my mind of negative thoughts and separate myself from negative people. My wife's battle against me was yet to be won.

I hope this book will encourage someone else that there's hope, if one is willing to acknowledge it, and realize that negative thoughts have no place in the courtroom.

CPSIA information can be obtained
at www.ICGtesting.com
Printed in the USA
BVHW031626231119
564518BV00020B/6/P